From the Shannon to the Ebro

The Limerick men who went to fight Franco

From the Shannon to the Ebro

PUBLISHED BY LIMERICK INTERNATIONAL BRIGADES MEMORIAL TRUST, 2014

Copyright (c) Limerick International Brigades Memorial Trust, 2014

First published in 2014 by Limerick International Brigades Memorial Trust

ISBN 978-0-9930447-0-0

The right of Limerick International Brigades Memorial Trust to be identified as the author of this work has been asserted by the Trust in accordance with the Copyright, Designs and Patents Act 1988

All rights reserved. No part of this publication may be reproduced, stored in a retrieval system or transmitted in any form or by any means without the prior written consent of the publisher, nor be otherwise circulated in any form or binding or cover other than that in which it is published and without a similar condition being imposed on the subsequent purchaser.

This publication has made every effort to respect all original material and copyright.

Cover design by Simon Donnelly.
Typesetting and design by Nóra Szekeres.
Printed and bound in Ireland by www.JustPrint.ie

Although every precaution has been taken in the preparation of this book, the publisher and author assume no responsibility for errors or omissions. Neither is any liability assumed for damages resulting from the use of this information contained herein.

CONTENTS

Acknowledgement i
Patrons ii
Foreword iii

Introduction

To the International Soldier Fallen in Spain	*Miguel Hernández*	13
Welcome by Limerick City and County Council Cathaoirleach	*Cllr Kevin Sheahan*	14
Limerick International Brigades Memorial Trust	*Jack Bourke*	16
The Memorial Stone	*Simon Donnelly*	18
The Limerick Mechanics' Institute & The Council of Trade Unions	*Mike McNamara*	20

The Spanish Civil War

The Spanish Civil War: An Overview	*Richard Baxell*	24
The International Brigades	*Ger McCloskey*	32
Exporting Ireland's Civil War	*Ruan O'Donnell*	36
What the Papers said	*John King*	38
Flowers for Franco	*Emma Gilleece*	49
Limerick and the Spanish Civil War	*Joe Malone*	52
Los Brigadistas en El Palacio de Deportes 1997	*John Liddy*	54

The Limerick Men

Jim Woulfe	*David Convery*	57
Joe Ryan	*Tom Collopy*	59
Gerard Doyle	*Mike McNamara*	63

From the Shannon to the Ebro

Emmett Ryan	*Alan Warren*	70
Paddy Brady	*Danny Payne*	74
Frank Ryan	*Manus O'Riordan*	78

The Spanish Civil War: An Anthology

'Farewell Spain' by Limerick writer Kate O'Brien	*Pamela Cahill*	93
Change is their memorial, who have changed the world	*Jane Bernal*	98
Heart of the Heartless World and Ringstead Mill	*John Cornford and Margot Heinemann*	104 105
From Limerick to Brunete: the Curious Story of George Nathan	*Melody Buckley*	106
Ned Vallely aka Peter Brady	*Ger McCloskey*	110
Reginald Watkins	*Bill Watkins*	111
Irish Women's Admirable Involvement in the Spanish Civil War	*Muireann Hickey*	112
Spain's Civil War Legacy	*Michelle O'Donnell*	115

De Profundis	*Federico García Lorca*	123
Contributors		127

Acknowledgments

The members of the Limerick International Brigades Memorial Trust wish to acknowledge the wonderful support received from the many institutions and individuals listed below. In addition, we wish to publicly thank all those, too numerous to mention, who provided moral or financial support at different times and helped us to sustain the effort and realise our goals. We wish to thank those who contributed articles for this publication and all those who helped with the mounting of the various events over our commemorative weekend.

We operate under the auspices of Limerick Trades Council and are indebted to them for the support they provided. LIBMT is based at the Mechanics' Institute and the Institute's encouragement and support has been significant.

We wish to make reference to the members of the former Limerick City and County Councils and thank them for the mature and generous manner in which they embraced the proposal to commemorate these men. We also wish to thank Mr. Conn Murray and the officials at Limerick City and County Council for their guidance and support in relation to the Memorial and engaging with us in a genuine sense of partnership.

Limerick City of Culture 2014 has been a very good supporter and we wish to thank them and to also congratulate them on the wonderful work they are doing in supporting and promoting the creative and culturally dynamic aspects of Limerick and its citizens.

We wish to thank the following for their kind support:

Tony Bennett	*Frontline EMS*	*John King*	*Shamie Quin*
Sonia Boue	*John Gavigan*	*Cllr Joe Leddin*	*Marie Quinlivan*
Phil Bourke	*Paul Gavin*	*Kathleen Leddin*	*Des Ryan*
Dolores Brazil	*Eugene Griffin*	*Paddy Lynch*	*Eamonn Ryan*
Victor Brown	*Michael Halpin*	*Katie McCloskey*	*Michael Ryan*
Ursula Callaghan	*Ian Hamilton*	*Margaret McEvoy*	*Peter Ryan (decd)*
Calton Books	*Tomas Hannon*	*Barry McLoughlin*	*Al Ryan*
Kevin Clancy	*Clare Hartigan*	*Elaine McNamara*	*Charlotte Ryan Whetton*
David Convery	*Maureen Hobbins*	*Anne Madden*	*Diarmuid Scully*
Josephine Cotter-Coughlan	*Frank Hough*	*Gabi Martin*	*Cllr John Sheahan*
Michael Cowhey	*John Hunt*	*Deirdre Minogue*	*Tom Shortt*
Helen Creed	*Mary Hurley*	*Mother Jones Comm. Cork*	*Jessie Skehan*
Sean Curtin	*Nora Hurley*	*Conn Murray*	*The George Hotel, Limerick*
Mary Davis	*ICTU*	*Eddie O Neill*	*Alan Warren*
Sheila Deegan	*Andy Irvine*	*Harry Owens*	*Barry Wharton*
Louise Donlon	*Liam Irwin*	*Amina Parkes*	
Mike Finnan	*Carol Jacobs*	*Pery's Limerick Hotel*	
Al Fitzgerald	*L and M Keating*	*Paul Quin*	

Patrons of LIBMT

Andy Irvine

Andy Irvine occupies a unique place in the musical world, plying his trade as an archetypal troubadour, with a solo show and travelling lifestyle that reflects his lifelong influence, Woody Guthrie. Few others can equal his repertoire; Irish traditional songs, dexterous Balkan dance tunes, and a compelling canon of his own material that defies description. Andy has formed or played with many legendary Irish music groups including Sweeney's Men, Planxty, De Dannan, Patrick Street, and Mozaik. He has also worked with other luminaries of Celtic music including Dick Gaughan, Paul Brady, Donal Lunny and John Doyle and has produced a number of solo albums. He continues to perform internationally with Mozaik and the reformed Patrick Street.

John Liddy

John Liddy, Poet, was born in Youghal, Co Cork, Ireland (1954), grew up in Limerick, took a degree in the University of Wales and works as a teacher in Madrid. His collections include Boundaries (1974, Jane Hunt/ The Limerick Leader), The Angling Cot (1991, Beaver Row Press), Song of the Empty Cage (1997, Lawping Press), and Wine and Hope/Vino y Esperanza (1999, Archione Editorial Madrid), Cast-a-Net (2003, Archione Editorial Madrid), The Well: New and Selected Poems (2007, Revival Press). His most recent book is Gleanings (2010, Revival Press). John is the founding editor along with Jim Burke of The Stony Thursday Book, one of Ireland's longest running literary reviews, along with Cyphers. He was Limerick City of Culture writer-in-residence for the month of July 2014.

Foreword

This publication is timed to coincide with the unveiling of a memorial to the Limerick men who fought with the International Brigades in the Spanish Civil War. The role played by these men in one of the most important events in the 20th century is commemorated throughout the world and it is fitting that they be remembered at home. The members of the International Brigades went to Spain in pursuit of an ideal. They knew the importance of their cause and believed that there were certain things worth fighting for.

It is not our intention in this book to provide a scholarly account of particular events or of the lives of people involved in the Spanish Civil War. These aspects are more than adequately catered for elsewhere. Rather, we hope, through a number of different articles from various contributors, to provide some background into why and how the project developed, to offer some colour and insight into the prevailing mood at the time and, most importantly, to flesh out the lives of the men whom we are commemorating and to record their sacrifice for posterity. Many of the contributors are eminent published authors while others have never before seen their efforts in print.

In the following pages, we endeavour to provide context and substance to the men's stories. It is not our purpose to glorify them or their deeds. They were ordinary men involved in extraordinary events. However, as the French philosopher Paul Ricoeur wrote "to die forgotten is to die twice" and we in the Limerick International Brigades Memorial Trust (LIBMT) are committed to ensuring that they are commemorated in their native place.

The LIBMT is comprised of a broad cross-section of people who came together to pay homage to these men. We were obviously motivated and inspired by their selfless action in volunteering to fight fascism in Spain in the 1930s but also we believe that their efforts have a resonance for the ages. Commemorating these men is not an exercise in nostalgia but serves as a constant reminder of the fragile nature of democracy.

It has been very heartening to us in LIBMT that Limerick, in embracing this project, has demonstrated an open and generous spirit towards these men whose loyalty to the Spanish Republican cause was very much a minority- held view in the Limerick, or indeed, in the Ireland of the 1930s. These men, in the choices they made, stood apart from the prevailing political, social and economic conventions of the time, and history has vindicated their stand. Others, who were encouraged and swayed by swollen and exaggerated misrepresentations of events in Spain, made different choices and many of them, to their credit, went on to fight fascism in subsequent wars.

As people who live and work in Limerick today, we understand and appreciate that we are part of a progressive and tolerant community that accommodates and celebrates diversity. We wish to record our thanks and appreciation to the Limerick City and County Council officials and political representatives for their unstinting support and encouragement. We regard the Council as our partners in this effort and their involvement in the project reinforces our belief that Limerick is proud of its strong tradition of working-class activism and these men are very much of that tradition.

The Trade Union movement at Trade Council, Union and individual level has provided very significant support and without their active participation it would not have been possible to undertake this project. The Mechanics' Institute has been our physical and spiritual home for the duration of the project and we owe a huge debt of gratitude to the Limerick Trades Council, Mike McNamara and his colleagues.

We wish to acknowledge and publicly thank the Limerick City of Culture Project for their financial and moral support. Since Limerick was designated as Ireland's City of Culture for 2014 we have witnessed an explosion of cultural activity and the growth in confidence of various groups, and the increased appetite for cultural offerings bodes well for the future.

Finally, we thank the myriad of people and organisations that have provided moral, financial and practical support to our project. It would be remiss not to mention Ger McCloskey who has been the inspiration and driving force behind this effort since the beginning and has persevered to see its realisation. We believe that this Memorial will serve to remind people and make them aware, not just of the sacrifices made by these Limerick men but also the cause they served and were prepared to die for.

"You can go proudly. You are history. You are legend."
(La Pasionaria)

Jack Bourke
Chairman LIBMT

From the Shannon to the Ebro

INTRODUCTION

From the Shannon to the Ebro

Al soldado internacional caído en España

To the International Soldier Fallen in Spain

Si hay hombres que contienen un alma sin fronteras,
una esparcida frente de mundiales cabellos,
cubierta de horizontes, barcos y cordilleras,
con arena y con nieve, tú eres uno de aquellos.

Las patrias te llamaron con todas sus banderas,
que tu aliento llenara de movimientos bellos.
Quisiste apaciguar la sed de las panteras,
y flameaste henchido contra sus atropellos.

Con un sabor a todos los soles y los mares,
España te recoge porque en ella realices
tu majestad de árbol que abarca un continente.

A través de tus huesos irán los olivares
 desplegando en la tierra sus más férreas raíces,
abrazando a los hombres universal, fielmente.

If there are men who contain a soul without frontiers,
 a brow scattered with universal hair,
 covered with horizons, ships, and mountain chains,
 with sand and with snow, then you are one of those.

Fatherlands called to you with all their banners,
 so that your breath filled with beautiful movements.
 You wanted to quench the thirst of panthers
 and fluttered full against their abuses.

With a taste of all suns and seas,
Spain beckons you because in her you realize
 your majesty like a tree that embraces a continent.

Around your bones, the olive groves will grow,
unfolding their iron roots in the ground,
embracing men universally, faithfully.

__Miguel Hernández__
English Translation By Tom Clark

Miguel Hernández was born in 1910 in the town of Orihuela, near Murcia, in south eastern Spain. On the outbreak of the Civil War, Hernández joined the Republican forces fighting Franco. He travelled extensively organising cultural events and conducting poetry readings for soldiers on the front lines, and when necessary, dug ditches or defended positions. He gained recognition as one of Spain's foremost poets.
His commitment to a democratic Spain resulted in his being sentenced to death by Franco after the war. The sentence was commuted to 30 years in prison. Years of war and struggle had left him weakened, and Miguel Hernández died in prison of tuberculosis in 1942.

Welcome by Limerick City and County Council Cathaoirleach Cllr Kevin Sheahan

Cllr. Kevin Sheahan, Cathaoirleach, Limerick City and County Council.

INTRODUCTION

I would like to welcome visitors to Limerick on the occasion of the unveiling of a memorial to the Limerick men who fought in support of Republican Spain during the bitter Civil War from 1936 to 1939. It was a seminal time in Europe and here at home the prevailing sentiment was very much in favour of Franco and the Nationalist side. The men who fought with the International Brigades are commemorated around the world and it is fitting that those six ordinary Limerick men who found themselves in extraordinary circumstances now be remembered in their native place. It should also be said that a number of Limerick men who travelled to Spain in support of Franco subsequently fought fascism during the Second World War and they are also remembered on this occasion.

These six Limerick men are from an ancient place with a proud and turbulent history. For Frank Ryan and Jim Woulfe, County Limerick was their playground, a place of rural charm and great beauty with a gently undulating landscape that varies from the mountains of Ballyhoura in the Golden Vale to the Shannon Estuary. Limerick City, with a charter older than London and a history peppered with settlements, sieges and a stubborn resolve, was home to Gerard Doyle, Joe Ryan, Emmett Ryan and Paddy Brady. Their Limerick has undergone a process of continuous change from its early days as a Viking settlement to its capture by the Anglo Normans and transformed itself from a medieval city to a Georgian metropolis and from a Victorian municipality to a 21st century economic powerhouse.

In contrast to the 1930s, all of Limerick today is diverse, multicultural and confident; embracing change with a revitalised sense of pride in place. It is now vibrant and progressive as the base for leading international companies with a renewed sense of community in its towns and villages, an energetic student population and a thriving arts community. Indeed, it could be said Limerick is now undergoing something of a renaissance since its designation as National City of Culture 2014.

This designation has provided us with the opportunity to support hundreds of distinct and exciting projects including the commemoration of the men who fought with the International Brigades in Spain. More importantly, the designation has encouraged community activism and facilitated the putting in place of structures and processes which will ensure that in future years a legacy will remain from this important cultural year.

The recent radical and immense transformation in local government that brought about the amalgamation of our former City and County Councils also presents new and exciting challenges for Limerick. In common with the rest of the country we have many pressing issues that require resolution. Most importantly, local government has been given a wider and clearer role in economic development as we plan towards realising our goals of Project Limerick – our 2030 vision which will guide the economic, social and physical development of Limerick over the years ahead.

All of these changes require creative thinking and a shared commitment to taking on what will be a demanding but nonetheless exciting role working for and on behalf of the people of Limerick.

This Memorial project is based on a voluntary effort by a committed group of people and Limerick City and County Council is happy to support them in their effort to commemorate the part played by Limerick men in momentous world events. The construction of a tribute to them is a welcome addition to the physical landscape of Limerick and I have no doubt will be thought provoking and informative for our citizens and tourists alike.

I trust our visitors will enjoy your stay in Limerick and we look forward to welcoming you back again and again.

Le Meas
Cllr Kevin Sheahan
Cathaoirleach, Limerick City and County Council

Limerick International Brigades Memorial Trust

It began in March 2012 with a journey to the annual commemoration ceremonies for the soldiers of the International Brigades held at Jarama in Spain and with the promise made that the significant role played by Limerick men in the fight for democracy would be commemorated at home. These men were participants in one of the most important political events of the 20th century and had been posthumously granted honorary citizenship by the Spanish Government for their role in the fight for democratic principles. The part they played is remembered in numerous countries around the world and elsewhere in Ireland and yet their story had still to be recorded in their native place. Something needed to be done about that!

So began a journey that brought together a group of people from different walks of life with different views of the world and with a variety of reasons for wishing to commemorate these men. It was a voyage of discovery on a number of levels: we began with the names of three Limerick men who fought with the International Brigades and, in the course of our research, discovered a further three. Whilst there was a large body of work relating to the significant role played by Frank Ryan with the International Brigades, there was scant information available regarding his Limerick comrades. Over time, we remedied that situation and now have a much fuller picture of the men who went to Spain and we are happy to share that knowledge.

What we learnt about these men was not always very flattering. By no stretch of the imagination could they be described as "paragons of virtue" or men who had lived unblemished lives. But what was captivating about them was that they chose to go to Spain in pursuit of an ideal against an overwhelming prevailing ethos, and history has vindicated the stand they took.

I suppose if there is a Don Quixote in this story, then it is Ger McCloskey. Ger is a very proud Limerick man and, in a general way, has been interested in the Spanish Civil War for many years. Following a visit to Jarama in 2012 with his good friend, Tom Collopy, he was moved by the sacrifices made by the men of the International Brigades in support of the legitimately-elected Republican government of Spain. He was particularly moved by the role played by Limerick men in the conflict and how they were commemorated in Jarama, and resolved that they be honoured at home.

Since then, Ger has managed to bring together a number of people drawn from various backgrounds who have worked together for the purpose of telling these men's stories to ensure that they are afforded proper respect for what they did and, in so doing, to enhance the reputation of Limerick and generally make people aware of its role in world important events. The people who answered Ger's call came from the University of Limerick, private business, public service and, very importantly, from the Trade Union movement. This group was very fortunate to come under the umbrella or auspices of the Limerick Trades Council, and the Mechanics' Institute provided it with the necessary accommodation and facilities.

The initial task was to establish, as best we could, how many Limerick men were involved. At one point, we were convinced we had identified seven men, but further research led us to conclude that Jim Tierney was a Dubliner. Our hopes for commemorating "the magnificent seven" were sadly dashed! So began the job of fleshing out the details of these men's lives, and the results are described elsewhere in this book. That journey, metaphorically, took us around the world to the US, Canada and Australia as well as closer to home.

One memorable day in August 2013, we travelled to Jim Woulfe's native Athea in West Limerick; Jim had fought and died at Belchite. We gathered with his family and friends at the home of nonagenarian, Nora Hurley, and her daughter, Mary, and swapped stories and reminiscences with Jim's grandnieces and their great friend and relation, John Hunt. John, who is well into his nineties, was on his annual pilgrimage to Ireland from his base in Chicago and recalled for us with startling clarity the circumstances of the time, the kind of world Jim Woulfe inhabited and the matters that influenced his political outlook. John himself was an old IRA man and had led an extraordinary existence and I look forward to some day reading the story of his life. There were numerous such encounters along the way, poignant and funny and all memorable. What is clear from our research and conversations is that there were no happy endings for these men, those who survived endured hard times and were largely forgotten.

LIBMT Exec. Committee. Left to right: Ger McCloskey (PRO), Emma Gilleece (Exec Off.), Jack Bourke (Chairman), Tom Collopy (Sec.), Mike McNamara (Vice Chairman) Other members of the Committee are: John Cantillon, Nick Condon, Micheal O Flynn, Shane MacCurtain, Dr. Cinta Ramblado

In relation to the form of commemoration we should put in place, the view taken was that the construction of a Memorial would be a fitting tribute to these men. The decision was made to commission a tasteful piece of sculpture which would reflect these men's sacrifice but would also enhance the visual appeal of our city and fully complement the city's existing and proposed programme of public art. We engaged the services of a young Limerick artist, Simon Donnelly, and he has brought great imagination and energy to his task.

We felt that we should also celebrate the lives of these men by establishing an annual cultural event in Limerick. Such an event would consist of debate and discussion on important historical and topical issues in the socio/political spheres as we believe that Limerick is a natural place for debate and reflection on such matters given its history of labour activism. We also felt that such an event should have the capacity to attract visitors to Limerick. In particular, we were anxious to promote stronger ties with Spain and the Spanish-speaking world and make Limerick a national hub for such interaction.

We were very fortunate that from the beginning the former Limerick City and County Councils were supportive. We were not interested in trying to convince people of the rights or wrongs of stances taken in 1930s Limerick. We felt that the Limerick of today should be prepared to acknowledge all aspects of its history and, after a process of dialogue and discussion, all political parties supported the case for commemorating these men. The positive engagement by the politicians gave us great encouragement, and the follow-up involvement by the Council officials was wholehearted and unstinting. The City Council offered to locate the Memorial in the precincts of the City Hall, and, in a real sense, they became our partners.

Our efforts, fortunately, coincided with the Government decision to designate Limerick as Ireland's City of Culture for 2014. We discussed our proposed plans for the commemorative weekend with the relevant voluntary group within the City of Culture, made our submissions and were approved support. This enabled us to plan our events with confidence in the knowledge that our own fundraising would be matched. We have had a good relationship with the City of Culture organisation and they have been very supportive of our efforts.

By and large, our efforts have gone smoothly but not without some hiccups along the way. We have a good network of local individuals and organisations that help each other and the support of the Trade Union family has been of tremendous benefit. We are looking forward to unveiling the Memorial on the 14th September and are busy preparing for that and the related events going on in Limerick over that weekend. We look forward to welcoming our visitors and guests and trust they will enjoy their time in Limerick.

Jack Bourke
Chairman

The Memorial Stone

by Simon Donnelly

I was delighted to be given the commission by the Limerick International Brigades Memorial Trust to design the stone that for the next hundred years or more will stand as a testament to the six men who left Limerick and joined the International Brigades in their stand against fascism.

All Civil Wars are the worst of wars, but the Spanish Civil War was to be a warning to all nations of what was to come. As its society divided and formed both right and left-wing camps, each developed separate and different ideals. The Nationalists became more and more entrenched in their views. Unwilling to accept the elected Republican government and with the aid of other European fascist governments, they began the attack on the Republican forces, and, in so doing, on the volunteers of the International Brigades. Within the Brigades were the six Limerick men, Paddy Brady, Gerard Doyle, Frank Ryan, Joe Ryan, Emmett Ryan and Jim Woulfe. I can't pretend to be able to imagine what they were individually thinking when they made their decision to fight. I wonder were there late night discussions on the evils of fascism? Did they roll out some old school maps of Spain and try to pronounce the place names? Were they angry at the Irish Church for its support of Franco, did they laugh and feel the excitement of the adventure, and did they fear the ultimate outcome of their decision? But as the six set off on their journey, I hope through my design in the immovability of stone to reflect the permanence of their opposition to the evil of fascism.

The Stone:

So the stone becomes real, solid sandstone standing 7"x2.5"x2" cut from a quarry in Donegal, transported to Limerick to be carved and shaped.

The design is chiselled in three layers letting the stone reveal the story. The first layer, the face layer, I kept as smooth and cold as possible. This is to reflect the dominance and functionality of the Fascist architecture of the time: symmetry and clean lines. But in this layer, you start to see cracks appear, small and large. It is as if history is forcing its way out from inside the stone. The unmarked graves cannot be hidden forever, as if the past needs to be acknowledged before we can move on.

In the second layer, I use the pre-Christian symbol of the Triskel. The Christians also saw the power in this symbol and adapted it as a representation of eternity, but I prefer the fact that those who went before took with them its true meaning, leaving us with its beauty and mystery. It is this beauty and mystery that has the power to knock over fascist dictatorships and instil hope and belief in future mankind.

The third and deepest layer is a representation of the ruins of Belchite. I have taken a piece of decorative stone carving that I saw in the rubble of Belchite. It is, perhaps, the corner of the property of a well-to-do merchant of the town or a tiny piece of a door frame to the Doctor's surgery, who knows? But I have hidden it behind the first layer, the coldness of fascism, and then, behind the second layer, the rebirth in the Triskel, to show it can take years of a craftsman's hands to produce such beauty and a minute to destroy it with the ugly weapons of war. This layer is mankind's choice. This is where the Limerick men made their choice and final stand.

The Tri Star.

This is cast in bronze, symbolically using spent bullets and shell cases gathered from each Spanish Civil War battle site where these men fought and died. This is their symbol, their compass and light to unite under, and so I have placed it high in the centre of the stone above their names.

The Base. A single flat stone.

I wanted to use the Celtic (Knot) weave, so I went looking for the right intricate design and found it in the unique weave of Nick Tweddle, a Scottish artist. I have used his inspirational design around the base to frame the stone.

I would like to say a special thanks to Ger McCloskey and the committee members, and also to Ian Hamilton, Stonemason.

Finally, I hope that by erecting the Memorial here in Limerick, we honour those who laid down their lives in far-off fields, and by placing it close to the river, we invite those from far-off fields to join us, the people of Limerick, in the celebration of freedom and life.

Simon at work.

The Limerick Mechanics' Institute & The Council of Trade Unions

Before the concept of public libraries in Britain and Ireland, there was not much available to the working classes by way of further education. Most working-class people left school early to assist with the rearing of younger children and often worked for a meagre wage in order to augment the over-stretched wages of a parent or older sibling. Often living in very poor conditions in bad and overcrowded accommodation, the further education of children was merely a dream of how life could have been if circumstances had been different.

After the Industrial Revolution, the notion of adult education was born from the requirement of industrialists to have an educated workforce capable of learning new methods and techniques. It was from these ideals that the first Mechanics' Institute was established in Glasgow in 1823. While in the first years they were slow to develop, the Mechanics' Institute movement expanded rapidly between 1825 and 1828, and included among their classes was instruction in mathematics, geometry and lectures in all things technical.

The Mechanics' Institute system was the beginning of vocational education as we know it and was funded initially by employers, but later developed as a subscription-based facility where membership of the Craft Unions normally provided for entry into membership of the Mechanics' Institutes as a delegate member. With this membership came access to the many and varied lectures, classes and, of course, the newly-established libraries and reading rooms which contained several of the local and national daily newspapers. Unemployed members would often call in to "The Mechanics" and sign the idle book from which employers would consult with the officers of the Institute when they had a requirement for skilled workers of a particular trade.

According to Dr. Kieran Byrne, however, in his book *Mechanics Institutes in Ireland 1825-1850*, many of the institutes were in decline by 1828, arising mainly from

the fact that "the lecture method presumed a literacy that may not always have been forthcoming" and there was also the suggestion that in times of economic downturn, the unions found it difficult to collect subscriptions from unemployed members and were unable to pay their delegate fees to the Mechanics' Institutes.

The Limerick Mechanics' Institute was initially founded in 1825 but very quickly afterwards declined into obscurity as a result of differences between the local clergy and politicians who had been appointed to its board of management. In April 1829, the Craft Unions or Guilds as they were known came together and re-instituted the Mechanics' Institute which was then housed in an old building at number 6 Bank Place. The new rules provided for a non-political, non-sectarian organisation and persons unconnected with the organisation could not be included on the delegate board, thereby eliminating political or religious influence which had brought about its earlier demise.

The Mechanics' Institute has continued uninterrupted in Limerick since 1829, and has been to the forefront of almost every major political campaign, hosting great public marches in the city. Starting out at No 6 Bank Place, the Mechanics' Institute moved to No 19 Lower

Glentworth Street in the late 1800s and it was here in April 1919 that the Limerick Mechanics' Institute and the Limerick Council of Trade Unions made international headlines when, in response to martial law being imposed on the citizens of Limerick by the British Military Authorities, The Trades Council called a general strike during which they printed their own currency and their own newspaper, and became known worldwide as "The Limerick Soviet". In 1922, the Mechanics' Institute moved into No 6 Pery Square and, in 1940, they developed the gardens at the rear of the building and constructed an assembly hall. Unfortunately, in 1970, due to rising costs of heating and lighting and due to an increase in municipal rates along with the worsening condition of the building, the committee decided to sell the main building at 6 Pery Square. They moved their facility permanently to the hall on Hartstonge Street where they developed offices at the lower end of the building. The Mechanics' Institute continues to play a role in the political and social life of Limerick and is still engaged in the protection of workers' rights and worker education. The building also houses a small collection of Limerick Labour History material and continues the tradition of hosting lectures and workers' activism classes.

The Limerick Council of Trade Unions was founded by the combining together of the Craft Guilds of Limerick. At the outset, they were not allowed to meet in public as a result of the Anti-Combine laws (1799 to 1824). During the 25 years that these laws were in force, the magistrates in all parts of Britain and Ireland did their utmost with fines and floggings to wreck the unions. Despite those draconian laws, however, the tradesmen of Limerick founded the Limerick Council of Trade Unions in 1810. They embarked on a long and cumbersome struggle for improvements in their working lives and for the good of society generally.

During the time of the Anti-Combine laws, members of the trade unions met in secret at a place called "Paddy's Hedge" on the canal. This was a double ditch which ran from the city side of the lock at Maddens Bridge to Lower Park. No longer illegal after 1824, it is no coincidence that when the Mechanics' Institute in Limerick was set up it worked in unison with the Trades Council and has done so ever since. The Trades Council began to campaign on behalf of society generally and everyone from farmers to fishermen applied to join the Trades Council or to form a guild. The Bakers Guild and the Pork Butchers Society were two of the more well-off guilds at the time as their produce was the staple diet of the poor working families of Limerick and this helped to bring about almost full employment all year round.

What was to become the proudest moment in more than two centuries of organised Labour in Limerick, however, occurred in April 1919 with the establishment of what was to become known as "The Limerick Soviet" when the workers of Limerick took on the might of the British Military and even put down a challenge to the Central Bank of England by producing their own bank note currency, by way of promissory notes. For almost two weeks in April 1919, the Limerick Trades Council ran the city. They organised food and fuel supplies and published their own newspaper, events which attracted worldwide attention at the time.

Prior to the establishment of the Labour Court, the Limerick Council of Trades Unions together with the Limerick Employers Federation operated the Local Joint Conciliation Board for the amicable settlement of local disputes. The conciliation board operated in the city right up until the 1960s. The Trades Council played a major part in Limerick Civic life and they had nominated delegates on numerous municipal boards including the Limerick Harbour Board, the City and County development boards, the Limerick City and County VECs and the roads, housing, planning and environment boards at both the City and County Councils.

The Limerick Trades Council continues today to provide a platform for political and social awareness and campaigning, and for the education of workers. The Limerick Resource Centre for the Unemployed, which was set up by the Trades Council for the provision of training and assistance to unemployed workers, continues to flourish. While the economic circumstances of the past five years have resulted in a decline in trade union membership, the sharp practices of some of the more ruthless employers in recent times has brought about a new awakening of workers and a new level of interest in collective bargaining.

Mike McNamara
President
Limerick Council of Trade Unions

From the Shannon to the Ebro

THE SPANISH CIVIL WAR

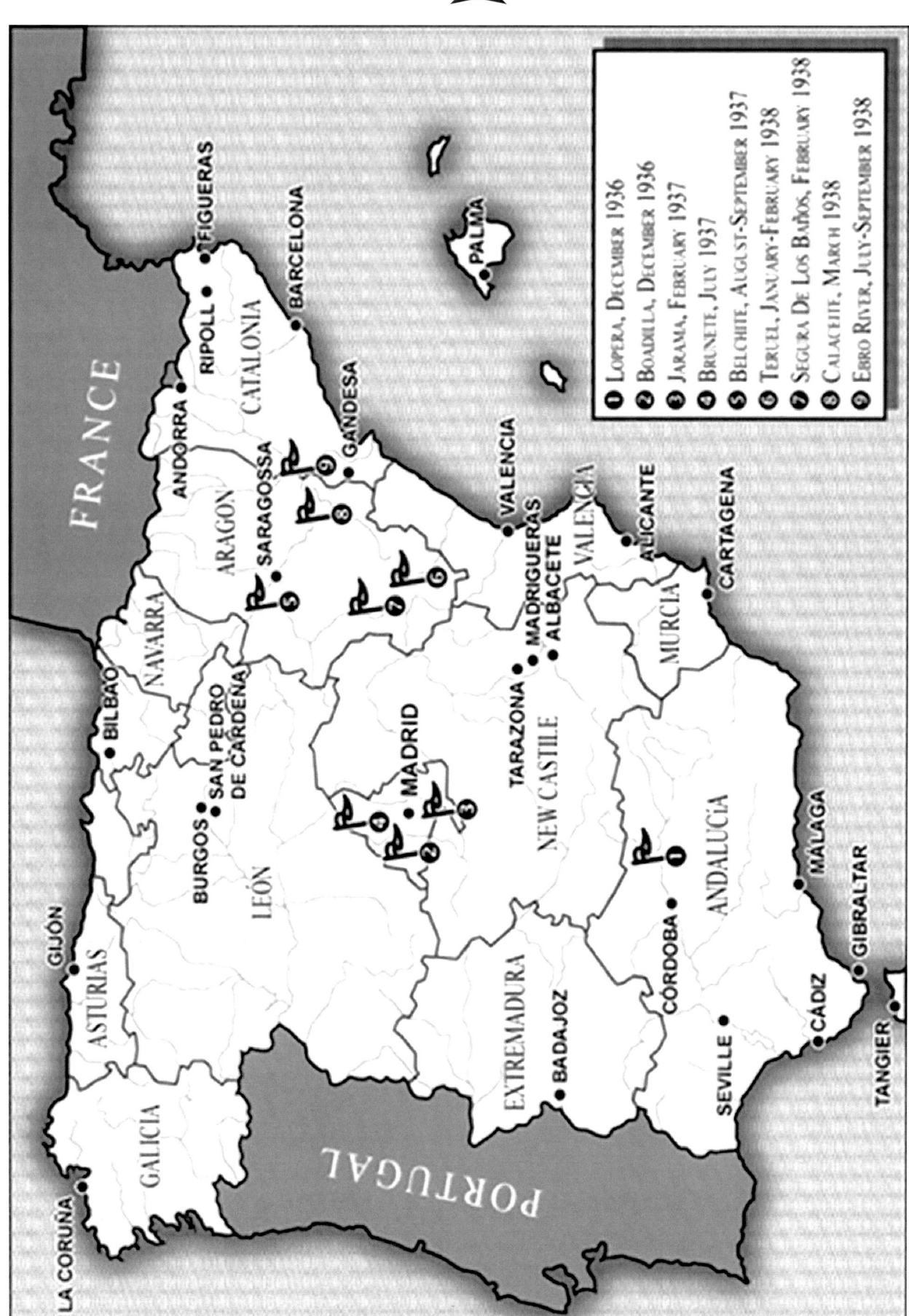

Timeline and Battle Sites where XV International Brigade was engaged

The Spanish Civil War: An Overview *by Richard Baxell*

Spain in 1931

Spain in 1931 was a country riven by inequalities. Still predominantly an agrarian country, traditional divisions endured between wealthy landowners, doggedly preserving their position, and a huge number of landless labourers and poverty-stricken smallholders, desperate to lift themselves from an existence of near-starvation. One of the largest landowners was the Catholic Church who, in addition to any theological motivations, were thus determined to maintain the status quo. Opposing the Church was the largest **Anarchist movement** in Europe, with a history of incendiary anti-clericalism. 'Spaniards' it was said, 'followed their priests either with a candle or a club'.

In the very few areas witnessing industrial change- chiefly Catalonia and the Basque regions- corresponding social and political change was largely absent. Aspirations by these regions for some degree of autonomy were bitterly opposed by the Spanish army who, fighting in Morocco to regain an empire which had been lost with the catastrophic defeat to the United States in 1898, strongly resisted any attempts to break up Spain. Large, powerful and extremely top-heavy in officers, the Spanish army had a tradition of involvement in politics; Primo de Rivera's military dictatorship had ruled Spain as recently as the 1920s. The dictatorship's legacy was a huge budget deficit at a time when the world was already sinking into economic depression, and its collapse spelled the end for the Spanish monarchy.

In April 1931, municipal elections were taken to be a plebiscite on the monarchy and the result was an overwhelmingly hostile vote against it. The King, **Alfonso XIII**, realising that he had lost not just the support of the populace but, crucially, the support of the military, fled Spain. Thus, on April 12, 1931, Spain's Second Republic, *la nina bonita*, was born.

The Second Republic

For many Spaniards the birth of the Republic was celebrated by exuberant public rejoicing; this seemed to many to signal the beginning of the end for the powerful Spanish elites, and to offer a relief for millions of landless peasants. However, attempts by the Republic to reform powerful institutions like the church and the army, at the same time as challenging entrenched economic interests in the landed, industrial and banking oligarchies, were never able to achieve the successes expected by the Republic's supporters on the left, while even limited reforms antagonised their opponents on the right. Separation of church and state, modernisation of the army and attempts to reform the deeply unequal distribution of the land were all regarded with horror by the established elites. In addition, attempts to meet the demands for regional autonomy from areas such as the Basque Country and Catalonia, further outraged the Spanish army.

The situation did not take long to escape from the government's rather tenuous control. Anarchist and other anti-clerical elements demonstrated their opposition to the Catholic Church by burning churches. The government, unwilling to use the forces of order against workers, some of whom were their own supporters, sat on their hands. If the government's reformist programme had not already alienated the army and church, the government's inability, or unwillingness, to control its supporters, guaranteed their opposition.

The elections of November 1933 saw a defeat for the republicans and socialists who fought the election as separate parties by a confederation of conservative and catholic parties, including the **Radical Party** and **CEDA**. Thus began the *bienio negro*, the black years, in which the reforms begun by the centre-left **Manuel Azaña's** government were at best abandoned or, in many cases, overturned. With the entry of CEDA into the government, perceived by opponents on the left as fascistic, the increasingly militant and revolutionary socialist party, the **PSOE**, responded in October 1934 with a general strike which, in some areas, escalated into armed insurrection. In Asturias, where miners were armed with dynamite, the rebellion endured longest. It was here too, that the governments' response was most vicious with Moroccan troops under the command of **General Francisco Franco** committing numerous atrocities. Several thousand were killed or wounded, including women and children, and thousands more were imprisoned.

The 1936 elections and the Popular Front government

The elections held in February 1936 saw a coalition of Spanish and Catalan republican and leftist parties, including the **PCE**, the **PSOE**, the **POUM** and the **Esquerra Republicana**, unite in a 'Popular Front', determined not to repeat the mistakes of the 1933 elections. Standing on a platform of reinstatement of the Catalan statute (with other regions such as the Basque regions and Galicia open to discussion), the revival of agrarian reforms and, significantly, amnesty, reinstatement and compensation for all political prisoners, they achieved remarkable success in gaining the electoral support of many Anarchists and won a narrow victory over the opposing coalition of the right.

The new republican government prepared themselves to revive the reformist programme of 1931, which had been abandoned by the conservative/reactionary government in1933. However, the unwillingness of revolutionary Anarchists and Socialists to participate in what they saw as an essentially bourgeois reformist government meant that the government lacked vital support from the left. At the same time, as political violence escalated, elements of the Spanish right, who had lost any faith in the Republic, prepared for war. As Paul Preston states:

> The elections marked the culmination of the **CEDA** attempt to use democracy against itself. This meant that henceforth the right would be more concerned with destroying the Republic than with taking it over. (Preston: Concise History, 59-60).

The military uprising

The murder of Calvo Sotelo, a prominent Catholic conservative politician, on 13 July 1936 by members of the Republican Assault Guard (itself a response to the murder of one of their comrades, Lieutenant Jose Castillo, the previous day) served as the perfect excuse for the leader of the plot, General Emilio Mola. On the evening of 17 July 1936, the military garrisons rose in Morocco, and the revolt quickly spread to the mainland. The rising began with army garrisons disarming loyal Republican Officers, then declaring the region for the Rebels. The rising was usually supported by Jose Antonio Primo de Rivera's **Falange** and the Civil Guard, who often acted on their own if the local town had no military garrison.

In Morocco, Mallorca, Old Castile, Navarre, Aragon and South Andalusia the rising was generally successful. However, in other areas, including the major cities of Madrid and Barcelona, the generals met with bitter and effective resistance from loyal members of the Civil Guard and Assault Guards, and from workers' militiamen who seized arms despite initial government opposition.

The uprising unleashed a terror in both Republican and Rebel held areas. In the 'Nationalist' sector, the military insurgents, aided by elements of the Falange, brutally demonstrated their determination to win by the cold and deliberate application of terror. Opponents of the rising, particularly members of the **PSOE** and the **PCE** or the **UGT** and **CNT**, but also many thousands of others with Republican sympathies were arrested and executed. In one of the most infamous events of the civil war, **Federico García Lorca**, the celebrated poet whose offence was to have Republican leanings, was arrested by a local member of the **CEDA** and murdered. Meanwhile, in the Republican sector, church burnings and the murder of suspected Rightists continued apace as militia units and 'uncontrollables' pursued their own revolutionary justice, despite attempts made by the government to contain the terror. The murder of 2,000 rightist prisoners in early November 1936 at Paracuellos del Jarama and the execution of Jose Antonio Primo de Rivera on the 20th were both used by the Nationalists to accuse the Republic of ' red barbarism'.

The onset of the Spanish Civil War

At this point the outcome of the rising was by no means certain. The Republicans held most of the navy, air-force and territory, including the capital and the vital industrial regions of the Basque Country and Catalonia. The rebels controlled the majority of the army, though the northern army, under General Mola, was paralyzed by a lack of arms and ammunition, and unexpected resistance from workers' militias, and the formidable **Army of Africa**, under the command of **General Franco**, was trapped in Morocco.

However, forces outside Spain decisively altered the progress of the conflict. Initially, following Jose Giral's desperate plea for assistance, **Léon Blum**, the French Prime Minister, had wished to aid the Republic and had authorised the sending of military aid, such as a number of aircraft arranged by **Andre Malraux**, a French pilot who organized a squadron of French pilots to fight for the Republic. However, following pressure from the British Foreign Secretary, Anthony Eden, and aware of the dangers of civil war in his own country should his government support the Spanish republic, Blum proposed an international agreement not to intervene in the conflict and a '**non-intervention**' **committee** was established in London to oversee the agreement. However, as the agreement was ignored from the outset by Germany and Italy and, later, by Russia, while other neutral countries such as Britain and the United States took no action against firms providing supplies to the Rebels, the agreement was singularly ineffective.

Meanwhile, despite initial reluctance to support what they saw as a risky enterprise (and despite their official adherence to the non-intervention agreement) both Hitler and Mussolini responded to requests from Franco for assistance by sending twelve Italian Savoia-Marchetti S.81 and thirty German JU 52s bombers, which allowed Franco to airlift the Army of Africa across the Gibraltar strait. The Army of Africa then advanced swiftly northwards towards Madrid and by August 10 they had reached Merida where they linked up Franco's southern zone with the northern zone of General Mola. The rebels then turned on the town of Badajoz, the capital of Extremadura. Despite a desperate defence, the town was captured and a brutal repression followed, during which nearly 2,000 people were shot. Stories and rumours of this savagery preceded the advance of the rebel army on Madrid, and worked considerably to the rebels' advantage. Militiamen, terrified at the prospect of being outflanked, retreated headlong, often dropping their weapons and ammunition, back along the main roads to Madrid, where they could be picked off with ease by the advancing rebel forces.

At the end of September, the rebel army made another detour to lift the siege of the city of Toledo which, crucially, allowed the defending Republicans time to prepare the defences in Madrid. After another massacre of militiamen, the march towards Madrid resumed. By November 1, the rebels had reached the south-west of Madrid adjacent to the Casa de Campo and University City. Here, at last, the advance was slowed by a defence established by militia units and the desperate population of Madrid. On November 10, 1936, the last ditch defence was joined by an international column

The Spanish Civil War: An Overview

of volunteers; the first of the International Brigades, determined to help ensure that Madrid would not fall, that the rebel army would not pass.

The war from the defence of Madrid to March 1939

In response to the desperate situation facing the Republic a true Popular Front government was formed in September 1936 containing, in addition to Republican parties, members of the PCE and PSOE. One month later, despite their ideological opposition, four representatives of the anarcho-syndicalist CNT also joined the cabinet.

By mid-October, the artillery fire of the approaching **Army of Africa** could be heard in Madrid and by early November elements of the Nationalist Army had reached the south-western suburbs. The Republican government was so convinced that Madrid would fall that, on 6 November, it left for Valencia, and placed the protection of the city in the hands of a military Junta de Defensa, under **General Miaja**.

However, helped by vital Russian military aid, the newly arrived 11th International Brigade and the Communist Party's **Fifth Regiment**, the population of Madrid embarked on a desperate defence, spurred on by the defiant speeches of **Dolores Ibarruri**, La Pasionaria. There was desperate hand-to-hand fighting as Moroccan troops almost reached the city centre, but the defenders drove them back. By the end of November,

the Nationalist attack was spent and the city, for the moment, held out.

The following month, in December, the rebels began an attempt to cut the Madrid-La Coruna road to the northwest of the capital. After heavy losses in fighting around the village of Boadilla del Monte, the attack was called off before, on January 5, the assault was renewed. During four days of fighting, for very little strategic gain by the rebels, each side lost in the region of 15,000 men. Casualties among the International Brigades were particularly high.

In February 1937 the rebels made a renewed attempt to surround Madrid by cutting the road to Valencia in the **Jarama valley** to the south of the Spanish capital. Republican troops reinforced by International Brigades, including British and Americans, were thrown in to the defence. Again the forces of the Republican Army held on desperately, allowing the rebels to make little progress and again the number of casualties was enormous. The Republicans lost perhaps 25,000 and the Nationalists 20,000.

On March 1, Franco agreed to a new two-pronged offensive to the east of the capital pressed upon him by Mussolini, flushed with the recent capture of Malaga by Italian forces. The plan involved an attack by Italian troops at Guadalajara, supported by Spanish forces moving on Alcala de Henares from Jarama. However, the Italians became bogged down by determined Republican resistance, aided by appalling weather conditions that prevented the rebel air-force from operating effectively. On March 12, the Republican forces, including Italian members of the International Brigades, launched a counter-attack. When the Nationalist offensive at Jarama failed to materialise, the Republicans routed the Italian forces. Mussolini responded furiously by declaring that Italian forces would remain in Spain until a Nationalist victory washed away the shame of their defeat at Guadalajara.

With Nationalist efforts to capture Madrid essentially defeated, the war moved to the north of Spain as Franco attempted to overcome Basque forces who, despite their Catholic beliefs, had remained loyal to a Republic which offered a level of autonomy fervently opposed by the rebels. As the Nationalist forces gradually closed on the heavily fortified city of Bilbao, the rebels launched an air attack on the ancient Basque market town of Guernica. In one afternoon of bombing, the undefended wooden town was razed to the ground by the German Condor legion. Attempts by the Nationalists to deny responsibility for the atrocity were quickly and effectively shown to be false and the bombing of **Guernica** took on a central significance in the war, immortalised by the famous painting by **Picasso**.

In May 1937 cracks in the Republican Popular Front coalition became significantly wider, when what was essentially a civil war erupted in **Barcelona**. Despite the inclusion of four anarchists into the Republican government, contradictions between Republicans, moderate Socialists and Communists on one hand and the revolutionary proletarian groups on the other had remained a burning issue for the Republic. The immediate catalyst of the May events was the raid on the **CNT**-controlled central telephone exchange ordered on May 3 by the **PSUC** police commissioner for Catalonia. The CNT and the **POUM** fought on for several days until the CNT leadership, only too aware that the civil war could only help Franco, instructed its militants to lay down their arms. Under strong pressure from the Communists, the Republic then set about ensuring the complete destruction of the POUM. In the ensuing crackdown the POUM leader, Andres Nin, was arrested and later murdered by the NKVD. Others members, including George Orwell, prudently went into hiding. The POUM was banned in June 1937, and moves were made to suppress the collectives and re-impose centralised government. By 1938 little of the autonomy granted by the Popular Front would remain.

The following month, in June 1937, Bilbao fell to the advancing Nationalist forces. The Republic responded by launching a major offensive at **Brunete** on July 6, designed to relieve pressure on the northern front and break through the rebels at their weakest point to the west of Madrid. However, despite initial Republican gains, Franco was able to bring his superior numbers to bear and gradually pushed back the republican forces.

With the failure of the Brunete offensive, Franco was able to continue with his northern offensive, and Santander fell to the rebels at the end of August. Again the Republicans tried to divert attention from the northern front by launching an offensive in **Aragon** aimed at capturing Saragossa. Though inroads into Aragon were made- International Brigades were heavily involved in capturing Quinto and **Belchite** despite heavy casualties- Saragossa remained in rebel hands, and the rest of the Basque regions and Asturias fell to the rebels by October 1937. The loss of the northern ports and the vital heavy industries was a crucial blow to the Republic.

Despite these losses the Republic launched a surprise attack in December 1937 and captured **Teruel**. In freezing winter conditions the Republic's best troops, including the International Brigades and the Communist 5th Regiment, fought desperately, but outnumbered they were unable to prevent Franco bringing his superior numbers of arms and men to bear. The Nationalists recaptured Teruel in February 1938.

The following month, on March 7, 1938, Franco launched a massive and well-prepared attack in Aragon involving 100,000 men, 200 tanks and over 600 Italian and German planes. What began as a series of break-throughs for the Nationalists swiftly became outright retreat for the exhausted Republican forces, as their lines virtually collapsed under the ferocious and well-supplied offensive. By April 15, the rebels had reached the Mediterranean and cut the Republic in two, and by the end of the month the rebels held a fifty-mile stretch of coast. Had Franco headed north into Catalonia he would probably have ended the war a year earlier than he did.

However, Franco's aim was not to defeat the Republic, but to annihilate it forever.

Three months later, in July 1938, the Republic launched what would become their last act when Republican forces advanced back across the River Ebro. A special Army of the Ebro was formed for the offensive, which was placed under the command of the Communist General Juan Modesto. But, as had happened too many times for the Republic, initial successes soon ground to a halt when faced with the nationalists' hugely superior numbers and armaments. The **battle of the Ebro** lasted for over three months until, bled to death, the Republican Army collapsed.

Meanwhile, events outside Spain had effectively sealed the Republic's fate when Czechoslovakia had been essentially "surrendered" to the Nazis at the Munich Agreement of September 29, 1938. Spanish premier Negrín's hopes of assistance from the western democracies were dashed but, nevertheless, Juan Negrín withdrew the International Brigades in October, gambling that pressure would be put on Franco to respond in kind, by sending back German and Italian troops. But it was too late. Supplied with fresh armaments from Germany, Franco's offensive of November 1938 sounded the death knell for the Republic and, by January, Franco had captured Barcelona.

On March 4, Colonel Casado, commander of the Republican Army of the Centre, launched a revolt in Madrid in an attempt to bring the war to an end. The revolt against the Republican government sparked off the second civil war in the Republican zone as Casado's forces battled with Communists who were determined to fight on. Over 200 were killed before Casado's forces gained control and an attempt was made to negotiate peace with Franco. However, Franco refused to negotiate and instead, on March 26, launched a gigantic and virtually unopposed Nationalist advance along a wide front. The following day Nationalists entered Madrid and, by March 31, 1939, all of Spain was in Nationalist hands. On April 1, 1939 Franco announced that the Spanish Civil War was officially at an end.

Refugees and internment

Following the fall of Barcelona in January 1939, a flood of desperate civilians including women and children flowed north towards France. Behind them came the retreating Republican Army covered by a rearguard composed of the Durruti Column and elements of the Army of the Ebro. Despite protests from the right wing press in France, the border was opened to admit them into France, where they were interned in **concentration camps** at Gurs, Argeles-sur-mer, Barcares and St. Cyprien. Conditions inside the camps were desperate, with shelter, supplies and medical care virtually non-existent. Strict military discipline prevailed, and those suspected to be Communists and Anarchists were taken to separate prison camps where they were held as prisoners under a regime of hard labour.

From April 1939 the Spanish Republican exiles were allowed the option to leave the camps, provided they obtained work with local employers or enlisted in labour battalions, the Foreign Legion or the French Army. Around 15,000 joined the Foreign Legion, including the elements of the **Durruti column** who were offered a choice between this and forced repatriation.

Following the fall of France in 1940 over 220,000 Spaniards were engaged in forced labour for French and German enterprises in France.

International Brigaders and Spaniards in the Second World War

Many of the International Brigaders from around the world continued their fight against fascism during the Second World War, though until the invasion of the USSR in 1941 official Communist Party policy was to regard the conflict as an imperialist war. And as 'premature anti-fascists', ex-brigadistas were not always admitted into the regular armed forces, despite their combat experience. Despite this, many served with distinction in the allied forces throughout the war in a wide variety of roles.

Many Spanish Republicans fought with the French army until France fell in July 1940. Of these, over 6,000 died and between 10,000 and 14,000 were taken prisoner when the Germans defeated France. Captured Spaniards were not treated as prisoners of war but sent to concentration camps, usually **Mauthausen**. As many as 30 000 Spanish refugees were deported from France to Germany, perhaps half of whom ended up in Nazi concentration camps.

During the course of the war thousands of Spanish Republicans fought with the allies in various theatres and a number fought in the Red Army and Soviet Air Force. A number of Basques fought in the Pacific with the US Army. Over 60,000 Spanish exiles fought with the French Resistance and more than 4,000 Spaniards took part in the Maquis uprising in Paris that began on August 21st 1944. Spanish Republicans were able to rejoice in a moment of triumph when the vehicles of the first units to liberate Paris carried Spanish Republican flags and bore the names Ebro, Madrid, Teruel and Guadalajara.

In total during the Second World War, 25,000 Spaniards died in concentration camps or fighting in armed units.

Courtesy of Abraham Lincoln Brigade Archives

The International Brigades *by Ger McCloskey*

International Brigades Farewell Parade
Barcelona 1938

In 1936, from 17-19 July, rebel generals along with a significant section of the military, revolted against the democratically-elected government of the 2nd Spanish Republic. The Popular Front government that had been elected in February 1936 on a broad programme of social reform of education, agrarian reform and increased wages was supported not just by communists, but by socialists, liberals, middle-class progressives, landless labourers, workers, Catalonians and Catholic Basques. The rebel coup was supported by a number of conservative groups, including: the Catholic Church, major landowners, Spanish Nationalists, monarchists such as the religious conservative Carlists, and the Fascist Falange.

Many foreigners who took part in the Civil War did so mostly on the fascist side. The Italians sent at least 70,000 men during the almost three years that the war lasted, the Germans 14,000 - mainly advisers, artillery and airmen, the Portuguese dictatorship 20,000 and there were 34,000 Foreign Legion and Moroccan troops. The largest volunteer force supporting Franco was the 600 Irishmen raised nationally by the fascist leader Eoin O'Duffy.

From the other side came the *International Brigades*, so called because their members came from some 53 countries; these were groups of foreign volunteers who fought on the Republican side against the Nationalist forces during the Civil War. The International Brigades were recruited, organized, and directed by the Comintern (Communist International) with headquarters in Paris. A large number of the mostly young recruits were left-leaning before they became involved in the conflict. Others, often affiliated with radical communist or socialist entities, joined the International Brigades believing that the Spanish Republic was a front line in the war against fascism. The French were the largest single foreign group (some 9,000); Germany, Austria, Poland, Italy, the United States, the United Kingdom, Yugoslavia, Czechoslovakia, Canada, Hungary and Belgium were also represented by significant numbers of volunteers.

There were seven brigades in all, and each one was divided into battalions by nationality (e.g., the French-Belgian Commune de Paris Battalion, the American Abraham Lincoln Battalion, and the British Battalion). The number of volunteers probably never exceeded 18,000 at any one time, but, in total, the number of volunteers, including a small number of women, reached about 40,000. The units represented the largest foreign contingent of those fighting for the Republic. The brigades were based at Albacete, and generally organised according to language. The XV International

Brigade was the main brigade to which the English-speaking volunteers were assigned. This was organised into the British Battalion, the two American Battalions – the Lincoln and the Washington – and the Canadian Mackenzie-Papineau Battalion.

Early volunteers were sent to Paris and over the Pyrenees by bus. However, after February 1937, the Non-Intervention Agreement forbade foreign volunteers or arms being sent to Spain. The thousands of troops and military equipment sent to aid Franco by Fascist Italy and Nazi Germany were generally overlooked, but it was far more difficult for aid for the Republic to get through. Volunteers had to leave their country secretly, pass through Paris where the Comintern organised their passage to Perpignan in the south of France. They then had to scale the heights of the Pyrenees by night to avoid detection. A number of volunteers died on this journey.

The International Brigades were used as shock troops by the Republican government, suffering appalling casualties with an attrition rate of over 80%. Most had never been in battle before, a few practice rounds fired whilst training was as close as they had been to the horrors of war that awaited them. They saw action in all the major engagements of the war, from the siege of Madrid until their withdrawal during the closing stages of the Battle of the Ebro. By the time of the Internationals' withdrawal, the Brigades were actually comprised of a majority of Spanish troops.

International Brigades Farewell Parade Barcelona 1938
Photo: Robert Capa

The Irish in the International Brigades.

Approximately 270 Irish volunteers fought with the International Brigades, of whom 60 died. Because of the secretive nature of volunteering, some used pseudonyms. Because the Republic lost the war, accurate records are not available so we may never know the exact number. As well as sympathy for the Spanish Republic, many Irish Republican volunteers were also motivated by enmity towards the Irish Brigade. This was a 600 strong force led by General Eoin O Duffy, the former Garda Commissioner and Blueshirt leader, who volunteered in late 1936 to fight on the Spanish Nationalist side. The atmosphere in Ireland, due to the Church's support of Franco, ensured that the majority of Irish people were pro-Franco. The war was seen as a religious rather than political conflict. "Red Rule in Spain" was the headline of the Irish Independent following the victory of the Popular Front Coalition. In September 1936, Cardinal MacRory, Primate of all Ireland, unequivocally declared the Church's support for Franco: "There is no room any longer for any doubts as to the issue at stake in the Spanish conflict. It is a question of whether Spain will remain as she has been for so long, a Christian and Catholic land, or a Bolshevist and anti-God one."

Some of these men on both sides saw the Spanish conflict as a continuation of Ireland's own Civil War including Republicans who relished the opportunity for another crack at their recent enemy, many of whom enlisted with O Duffy's Brigade; however, the Irish International Brigaders included many other strains of socialist and left-wing ideology. They fought for a variety of motives: anti-fascism, the defence of Spanish democracy, revolutionary idealism, and adventure.

Just under half were Communists, with many of these having a background in the general Irish Republican movement and particularly the Republican Congress. Frank Ryan was the de facto leader. He is quoted at the quayside on leaving for Spain:

> The Republican contingent, besides being a very efficient fighting force –every member of it having been in action – is also a demonstration of the sympathy of revolutionary Ireland with the Spanish people in their fight against International Fascism. It is also a reply to the intervention of Irish Fascism in the war against the Spanish Republic, which, if unchallenged would remain a disgrace on our people.

> We want to show that there is a close bond between the democracies of Ireland and Spain. Our fight is the fight of the Spanish people, as it is of all people who are victims of tyranny.

On arrival in Spain, the former I.R.A men did not require much training and went straight into battle on the Córdoba Front in the Christmas of 1936. They were led into their first battle which took place in an olive grove on the Córdoba Front by Kit Conway. They were then transferred to the Madrid Front, and at the end of January 1937, the badly-depleted unit was returned to base to join the newly-formed XV International Brigade. The Irish were split between the British Battalion and the Lincoln Battalion, in which they formed the "Connolly Centuria" or Column.

The old village of Corbera d'Ebre on Montera Hill has come to symbolise the tragedy of war. With a population in 1938 of almost 2,500 inhabitants, its ruined streets and houses nowadays bear silent witness to the violence and brutal consequences of air-attacks and artillery fire which the civil population suffered throughout the battle

The Irish fought in the Battle of Jarama where they lost 19 men, including the much-loved Kit Conway. The Irish also fought in the Brunete offensive of July 1937 and the Aragon offensive of August 1937. In Aragon, the British and Irish Battalion were led by the Irishman, Peter Daly, and after his death during an offensive at Quinto, they were led by another Irishman, Paddy O' Daire from the Glenties area in County Donegal. The Irish also took part in the Battle of Teruel in early 1938. Frank Ryan was captured by Italian troops near Calaceite, Aragon, on the 26th of March 1938. The final battle in which the Irish fought was the Battle of the Ebro in July 1938. Just before the withdrawal, Jack Nalty was killed on the 23rd of September.

On September 21st 1938, whilst the decisive Battle of the Ebro was still being fought, the Republican Prime Minister, Dr. Juan Negrin, in a desperate last effort to win the support of the Western governments, announced the withdrawal of the International Brigades from Spain in the hope that this would lead to the withdrawal of the Italian, German and Portuguese troops who were fighting for Franco. The actual evacuation of the International Brigaders was very difficult. Whilst 4,640 were repatriated, about 6,000 volunteers remained demobilised in Catalonia. As the region fell, the Communist Party called on the remaining International Brigaders to re-enlist. Eighty percent did so, fighting in the desperate rearguard actions as the Republican forces and hundreds of thousands of refugees fled towards the border. On 9 February, the International Brigaders were among the last Republican troops to cross into France". (AD 1)

At a parade in Barcelona given in their honour, just months before Franco came into control of the entire country and a long dark period of repression would begin, Dolores Ibárruri, La Pasionaria, gave the farewell address which finished with these famous words:

> We shall not forget you; and, when the olive tree of peace is in flower, entwined with the victory laurels of the Republic of Spain --- return!
> Return to our side for here you will find a homeland --- those who have no country or friends, who must live, deprived of friendship --- all, all will have the affection and gratitude of the Spanish people who today and tomorrow will shout with enthusiasm --- Long live the heroes of the International Brigades!

I would like to leave the final summation to the historian, Andy Durgan:

Despite the obvious weaknesses of the International Brigades' politics, for the left today they remain one of the most impressive and heroic examples of working-class internationalism and anti-fascism. As US volunteer and life-long Communist, Alvah Bessie, wrote, 'In the history of the world there had never existed a group of men like this...an international army formed...by volunteers from all walks of life. The actual existence of this army...was a guarantee of the brotherhood of the International working class, the definitive proof that [the workers] have a common interest and obligation'. This internationalism could not have contrasted more strongly with the treacherous policies of the bourgeois democracies and their political supporters, both left and right, who preferred the Republic to fall rather than themselves make a stand against fascism. Despite being relatively few in number, the International Brigades played a relatively important role as shock troops. Their political commitment and revolutionary consciousness, despite the treacherous role of their Stalinist leaders, were central to their effectiveness and for this they paid a heavy price. The fact that many International Brigaders were later persecuted by democratic governments, and by fascist and Stalinist regimes alike, is the clearest testimony to the example they provide to anyone who seeks to rid the world *of injustice.*" (AD 2)

With thanks to Andy Durgan - AD 1& 2 extracts from Freedom fighters or *Comintern army*", and David Convery for his assistance.

The International Brigades

Exporting Ireland's Civil War

by Ruan O'Donnell

The advent of the Spanish Civil War stirred Irish society in a manner not witnessed since the Great War when hundreds of thousands were mobilized by virtue of military engagement or alterations to the wartime economy. The cause of Republican Spain, however, also recalled the less numerically significant but politically profound raising of the pro-Boer Commandoes that went to Southern Africa to defend the Orange Free State and Transvaal from naked British imperialism. The challenge of defending democracy in 1930s Spain from opportunist attack by local and international forces of reaction was met by the followers of James Connolly. Those who joined the XVth International Brigade and other volunteer formations faced, at least nominally, other Irishmen who rallied to Generals Mola and Franco as 'Blueshirts' and in so doing extended Ireland's Civil War to a Spanish arena.

Attack on Strand Barracks Limerick July 1922
Photo courtesy of Sean Curtin, Limerick: A Stroll Down Memory Lane

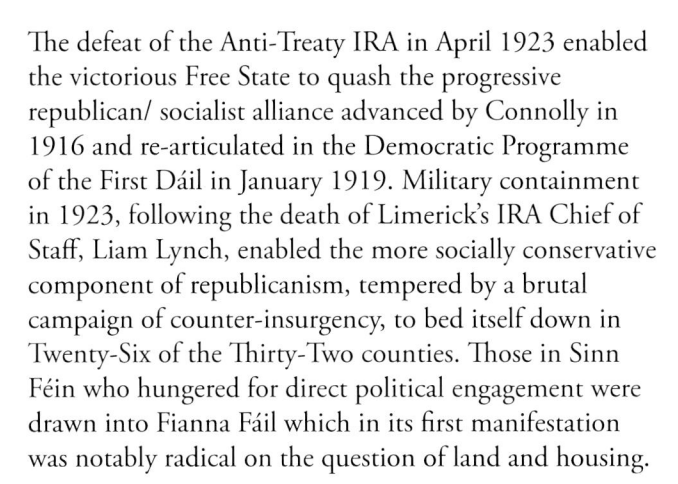

The defeat of the Anti-Treaty IRA in April 1923 enabled the victorious Free State to quash the progressive republican/ socialist alliance advanced by Connolly in 1916 and re-articulated in the Democratic Programme of the First Dáil in January 1919. Military containment in 1923, following the death of Limerick's IRA Chief of Staff, Liam Lynch, enabled the more socially conservative component of republicanism, tempered by a brutal campaign of counter-insurgency, to bed itself down in Twenty-Six of the Thirty-Two counties. Those in Sinn Féin who hungered for direct political engagement were drawn into Fianna Fáil which in its first manifestation was notably radical on the question of land and housing.

The avowedly revolutionary remnant of Sinn Féin was further depleted when considerable numbers of the most militant IRA members broke away to form Saor Éire and then the much larger Republican Congress. Led by ex-IRA leader, Frank Ryan, a charismatic, respected and articulate Limerick man, the Republican Congress openly challenged the temporal authority of the Catholic Church and the legitimacy of former comrades who had settled into what they believed to be an unhealthy co-existence in Leinster House with arch enemies of the Irish Republic proclaimed in 1916.

The threat posed by domestic ultra-conservatives aligning as the quasi-fascist 'Blueshirts', confirmed that Ireland did not stand immune from potentially disastrous political trends on the Continent. Tom Barry and other traditional IRA commanders confronted Eoin O'Duffy's 'Blueshirts', numbering many Civil War veterans, in the streets and fields. Republican Congress was drawn inexorably to Spain to confront the legions massing from North Africa, Italy and Germany to destroy the Spanish Republic. Whereas Barry reasonably argued that the migration of actual, former and potential IRA Volunteers to Spain weakened the republican cause in Ireland, Ryan averred that the early showing of armed fascism in Iberia demanded a response from those capable of making the crossing. Taoiseach, Eamon de Valera, another man with deep Limerick connections, attempted to prevent both Ryan and O'Duffy from complicating Ireland's vexed foreign relations. Ultimately, if often posthumously, the Brigadistas gained prestige.

Limerick was a county of intense political tradition. The 'Soviet' General Strike and transition from the War of Independence to a bitter Civil War in the heart of the 'Munster Republic' left deep scars on all its inhabitants. If a centre of strength for those who believed 'godless Communists' in Spain must be curtailed, it was also the cradle of a strong cadre of republicans, socialists, trade unionists and progressives whose commitment to defending democracy alongside comrades from many countries was vindicated by the cataclysm of the Second World War. This phenomenon clearly merits much further research and debate.

What the Papers Said *by John King*

An eclectic trawl through Press Archives for the period 1936-1939 examining aspects of the Spanish Civil War, the Irish Brigade, the International Brigades and the battle for public opinion.

Early Days

The Spanish Civil War started on 17th July 1936 and officially ended on 1st April 1939 with victory for General Franco and his insurgent forces. General Franco went on to rule Spain for the next 36 years.

Before the war started in July of 1936, the newspapers were carrying reports from Spain on a situation 'becoming hourly more serious', as reported in the *Irish Press* on Saturday 13th June 1936.

Irish Press Saturday13th June 1936.[1]

> **SOCIALIST—COMMUNIST CLASHES CONTINUE IN SPAIN**
>
> THE situation in Malaga, where a general strike and a conflict between Socialists and Communists have been in progress for the past few days is becoming hourly more serious, says Reuters' correspondent.

The war eventually broke out, initially in Spanish Morocco but quickly spread into the Spanish mainland and to the Canary and Balearic islands. The descent into war was widely reported in international, national and local newspapers.

Irish Independent Monday 20th July 1936.[2]

> **CIVIL WAR IN SPAIN**
>
> THE civil war which has been brewing in Spain ever since the triumph of the Left at the elections held last February seems to have broken out at last. During the past forty-eight hours there has been a

Limerick Leader Wednesday 29th July 1936.[3]

> **DESPERATE FIGHTING.**
>
> Reports from the South go to show that desperate fighting is going on without either side securing a decisive victory, so far. The insurgents, however, are in control of most of the Southern provinces.

The above report from the *Limerick Leader* of July 1936 describes the 'Desperate Fighting' ongoing in Spain. The next report on the same page, in the same column reports on a concern in local Catholic Church circles about 'mixed bathing' of men and women at a local swimming spot on the Shannon river, close to the City. This mix of reports shows that no matter what major events are happening overseas more immediate concerns will also feature in the local papers!

> **MIXED BATHING**
>
> —oo—
>
> **STRONG CONDEMNATION**
>
> A strong condemnation of mixed bathing was made by Rev. Father Fox, C.SS.R., in the course of an address to the members of the Arch-Confraternity of the Holy Family in the Redemptorist Church last night.

A Limerick connection through the Limerick Steamship Company was reported by the *Irish Independent* of Tuesday 4th August 1936 on the proximity of one of its vessels, the s.s. Clonlara, to the war action in the Mediterannean.

Irish Independent Tuesday 4th August 1936.[4]

> **IRISH VESSEL NEAR SCENE**
>
> **EYE-WITNESS STORY**
>
> ("Irish Independent" Special Representative.)
>
> Galway, Monday.
>
> AN eye-witness account of the bombardment of Algeciras in the Spanish civil war was given to me by Mr. McMillan, Montrose, Scotland, chief engineer of the s.s. Clonlara (Limerick Steamship Co.), which put

What the Papers Said

Hearts and Minds

As well as the actual war in Spain a 'war of words' was being fought in Ireland in the reports and commentary of the papers for the 'hearts and minds' of the Irish people. There were statements and comments from the Irish Government, from opposition parties, from trade unions, from republicans, from the Churches, particularly the Irish Catholic Church, from individuals supporting Franco and others supporting the Republican cause, and many more besides. These were in addition to the reports from the war zones being provided by the war correspondents and international news agencies such as Reuters and Associated Press.

The Irish Christian Front was set up and became a strong supporter of the Catholic position on the civil war. The Church saw the war as a 'crusade' to save Christianity from being overthrown by the 'Reds', whom the Catholic Church described as godless communists. *The Limerick Leader* of 26th September 1936 carried a strong line on this from Aodh de Blácam. He stated that 'for Irishmen (there is) only one answer' and that 'the liberty of the (Catholic) Faith' is the main target of the war, even if this required the imposition of a right-wing dictator in Spain. De Blácam, a writer and journalist with the *Irish Times* and the *Irish Press* was a noted supporter of the Franco side in the Spanish conflict. He engaged in a series of letters to the papers especially the *Irish Times* in August and September 1936 putting forward arguments in support of the insurgents and Franco.

Limerick Leader Saturday 26th September 1936.[5]

> **FOR IRISHMEN ONLY ONE ANSWER.**
>
> For Irishmen there is only one answer Our nation clung to the Faith and cheerfully went without material prosperity We all know that the world is ill-bought at the cost of the soul. Hence, if democracy is to perish and the Church is to be restored by a Dictator, we must bless that Dictator. The liberty of the Church is the supreme good to be sought in any civilisation.
>
> However, this extravagant position is not the real position. I have stated it simply to show that we ought to be unanimous and unhesitating in our moral support of the struggle for the Faith. The full truth is that the war for the liberty of the Faith is also a war for true social liberty. If the Right

The Primate of All Ireland, Cardinal MacRory, was also urging support for the Franco side to help save, as he believed, the Christian Church in Spain. The Cardinal described the Irish who supported the Republicans as 'misguided'. This was in response to the actions of Frank Ryan, from near Knocklong in County Limerick, and the others who had sent letters of sympathy and support to the Spanish, Catalan and Basque Republicans.

Frank Ryan responded with his own letter to Cardinal MacRory printed in the *Irish Times* in September 1936. He argued for the separation of political determination from religion and religious practice and argued on behalf of his own Catholicism. He concluded his letter with a strong message on the separation of Church and Politics.

The Irish Times Wednesday 23rd September 1936.[6]

> Finally, may I assure your Eminence that, as a Catholic, I will "take my religion from Rome," but that as an Irish Republican, I will take my politics neither from Moscow nor Maynooth?—Yours, etc.,
> FRANK RYAN.

Fighting in Spain

Franco was getting supplies of weaponry and soldiers from Italy and Germany. Russia was supporting the Spanish Government side. Many other countries including Britain and the USA had signed a 'Non Intervention' pact which should have meant no intervention on either side in the war. However, this pact didn't stop large numbers of volunteers signing up to fight in Spain from various countries around the world.

The hearts and minds debate in the Irish papers had continued with almost daily 'battles' to sway public opinion in support of one side or the other. From the early stages of the war, there were moves underway in Ireland to recruit volunteers to fight in the Spanish Civil War. General Eoin O'Duffy, leader of the Blueshirts in Ireland, was to the forefront in the formation of an Irish Brigade to go to Spain to help General Franco and the battle for Christianity.

Peadar O'Donnell, the aforementioned Frank Ryan, and others with Irish republican, socialist and left-wing political views, were canvassing support on behalf of the Republican (Government) side in Spain and seeking volunteers to fight with the 'International Brigades'.

The first Irish Volunteers were reported to be off to Spain as 'the advance guard for Gen. Owen O'Duffy's Irish Brigade', according to the *Chicago Daily Tribune* of 14th November 1936.[7]

The International Brigades were also attracting the support of well-known people such as Ernest Hemingway who was reported going to Spain in early 1937 to help the 'Red Forces'.

Irish Independent Friday 15th January 1937.[8]

> **TO FIGHT—OR WRITE?**
> New York, Thursday—Ernest Hemingway and John Dos Passos, well-known American authors, declare that they are going to Spain next month to give whatever help they can to the Red Forces. Mr. Hemingway says he will send dispatches to an American newspaper syndicate, and Mr. Dos Passos also intends to write about the civil war.—Reuter.

In Ireland, volunteers were signing up for O'Duffy's Irish Brigade or were aligning themselves with Frank Ryan in support of the Republican cause. The newspapers carried various snippets highlighting where individual Irishmen had left their jobs to fight in Spain.

Irish Press Tuesday 15th December 1936.[9]

Justice His Own Clerk

District Justice Kenny had to act as his own clerk at Rathkeale yesterday, the registrar, Mr. Daniel Ahern, having left for Spain to fight with General Franco's forces.

On the same day the *Irish Independent* reported on a vacancy that had come up in Bandon resulting from the Spanish conflict.

Irish Independent Tuesday 15th December 1936.[10]

A CORK VOLUNTEER

The Matron of the Bandon Cottage Hospital reported to the South Cork Board of Public Assistance that the temporary porter, Michael O'Connell, went off duty on November 26. He wrote to her as follows: "I am taking leave of absence from the above date, November 26, for at least 12 months. — Yours obediently, Michael O'Connell."

Mr. Crowley—He is gone to Spain.

Eoin O'Duffy's call to arms was reported in the *Irish Times* on 26th September 1936.

The Weekly Irish Times Saturday 26th September 1936.[11]

The following circular letter appeared in the *Morning Post* on September 17, and was stated to have been received by that paper from a reliable source. It was signed by Eoin O'Duffy, General, and reads:—

"THE IRISH CRUSADE AGAINST COMMUNISM.

"Phones:—City, 44458.
Blackrock, 445.
"12 Pearse street, Dublin.
"Director of Organisation—Eoin O'Duffy.
"Confidential Circular.
"A CHARA,—Your offer to join the Irish Brigade is accepted. Hold yourself in readiness to travel with first batch on short notice. Please treat this matter as strictly secret, in interest of Faith and country.—Mise le Meas,
"EOIN O'DUFFY, General

The bulk of volunteers left Ireland towards the end of 1936 as reported in the main national newspapers.

Irish Independent Monday 14th December 1936.[12]

HUNDREDS OF VOLUNTEERS SAIL

693 MEN LEAVE GALWAY

NORTHERN IRELAND'S QUOTA

EARLY MORNING DEPARTURE

A CONTINGENT of 693 men from all parts of Ireland left Galway early yesterday morning on board the tender Dun Aengus, and joined in Galway Bay a ship which will take them to Spain to fight with General O'Duffy's Irish Brigade.

Every county in the Free State was represented, and, in addition, there were 22 men from Northern Ireland. These volunteers, with the 100 who sailed from Dublin on Friday night,

Irish Press Monday 14th December 1936.[13]

IRISH DIVISION TO FIGHT FOR SPANISH GOVERNMENT

EIGHTY men left Ireland through the ports of Dublin, Belfast and Rosslare last week to fight against Franco

They will join the Republican Battalion which is being formed by Irishmen of the International Force in the service of the Spanish Government.

Not all the Irish Catholic Clergy supported the Franco side in the war and one priest with a strong Irish Republican heritage, Father Michael O'Flanagan, stood out. He frequently spoke on behalf of the Republican side in Spain, and in 1938 he was a speaker at an event in Dublin to commemorate the Irish volunteers who died fighting for the Republican cause. In his speech, he again argued that the fight wasn't about a particular religion but was about political determination and he drew on aspects of Wolfe Tone's political philosophy to make his point as reported in the *Irish Times* of the day.

Irish Times Saturday 12th November 1938.[14]

TONE'S AIM
"Tone's aim," he said, "was to unite the whole population of Ireland and to substitute for Catholic, Protestant and dissenter, the common name of Irishman."

Volunteers return to Ireland

Eoin O'Duffy's Irish Brigade returned to Ireland in June 1937 without having had much direct engagement in the battles of the civil war. Their return was a tense affair and O'Duffy complained bitterly that he and his fellow brigaders were being 'treated as criminals by an Irish Government' on their arrival into Dublin.

Irish Press Monday 22nd June 1937.[15]

IRISH BRIGADE HOME FROM SPAIN

ARRESTS FOLLOW SEARCH AT DUBLIN PORT

Mansion House Reception

WAVING the Tricolour and the flag of the Spanish Insurgents and singing verses of the National Anthem and "Faith of Our Fathers," 633 members of the Irish Brigade, headed by General O'Duffy, arrived from Lisbon on the S.S. Mocambique, a Portuguese liner, in Alexandra Wharf, Dublin, yesterday at

In September 1938, the Spanish Government as part of their 'war strategy' decided to 'stand down' the International Brigades. Their hope was that this action would help their overall position in the war, a hope that wasn't realised.

Irish Press Monday 21st November 1938.[16]

VOLUNTEER WITHDRAWALS.

The total number of volunteers of the International Brigade to be withdrawn from Government Spain under the League of Nations Volunteers Commission is 12,000, it was learned from a reliable source in Barcelona, states a Press Association Foreign Special message.

The volunteers represent 53 nations, and are stated to include 800 British, 350 Canadians, and 103 Russians.

Irish Press Monday 11th October 1938.[17]

MORE IRISHMEN KILLED

THE survivors of the 400 Irishmen who fought in Spain, under Major Frank Ryan, are expected to return to Dublin within a fortnight, according to a report supplied to THE IRISH PRESS.

Their losses were extraordinarily heavy—12 killed, 114 wounded, 12 captured. Eighteen were decorated wounds kilomet[...] before home [...] went ba[...] that Ma[...] Mr. M[...] of B Co[...] and la[...] organise[...] Party. The

Irishmen continued to return home through the remainder of 1938 as reported by the *Irish Independent* and *Sunday Independent* in late December of that year.

Irish Independent Tuesday 20th December 1938.[18]

Terence McCarthy, who gave up a window cleaner's round in London to fight in Spain, saw his mother and brothers again after nearly two years.

Sunday Independent 11th December 1938.[19]

BACK FROM SPAIN

Three members of the International Brigade who fought with the Reds in Spain—Messrs. T. O'Brien, J. Power, and M. Riordan—returned to Dublin yesterday. They were met at Dun Laoghaire by a guard of honour bearing Irish and Spanish flags. Later a procession, numbering between 300 and 400, formed up outside Westland Row station and, headed by a pipers' band, marched to Middle Abbey St., where a meeting was held. A strong force of Civic Guards accompanied the procession.

The meeting was addressed by Mr. T. Flanagan, who had returned from Spain some time ago, Father Ml. O'Flanagan, and Mr. J. Power.

War Correspondents

The Irish newspapers were receiving war reports from the various International Press Associations. Some of them had, at different times, their own correspondents in Spain whose job was to report back for their paper.

Among the war correspondents actually in Spain during the 1936-1939 period, were:

Lionel Fleming, Irish Times
Gertrude Gaffney, Irish Independent
MJ Buckley, Cork Examiner
Francis Mc Cullagh, Irish Independent.

L.T. Fleming was in Spain soon after the war began and had a number of articles in the *Irish Times* in September 1936.

Irish Times Wednesday 16th September 1936.[20]

> **WAR AGAINST CHURCH IN BARCELONA**
>
> **GREAT DIFFICULTY OF ARRIVING AT THE TRUTH**
>
> Soon after my arrival in Barcelona I was walking down the Ramblas with an English journalist, and, as we passed one of the ruined churches, I deplored the fact that so fine a building should have been destroyed so senselessly. "No doubt," he said, " but that church was held as a fort, and when it was burning we could not go within a hundred yards of it, because of the ammunition exploding inside." This journalist, who was in the city all through the rising, is a man of high standing, and I can think of no reason why he should wish to deceive me on this point. As a

The *Irish Times* attracted considerable criticism and threats from advertisers for Fleming's reports. His critics believed he was too close to the Republican side and wasn't giving a balanced view in his reports especially on the role of the Catholic Church.

Gertrude Gaffney, reporting in 1937 is much more aligned with the Franco and Church side as evidenced by her copy of June 1937.

Irish Independent Saturday 5th June 1937.[21]

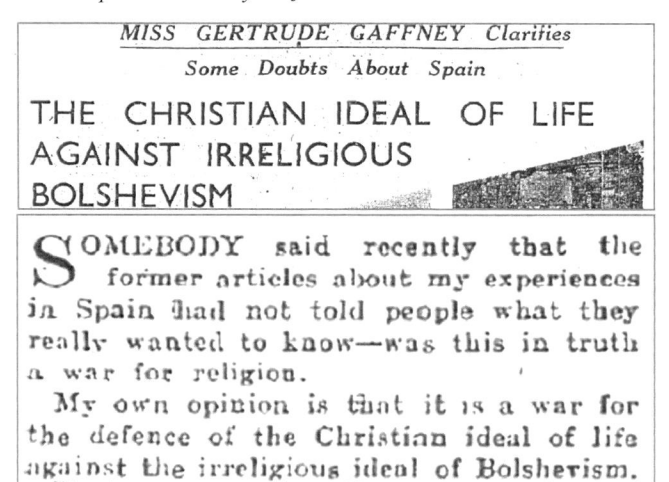

> **MISS GERTRUDE GAFFNEY** Clarifies
> Some Doubts About Spain
>
> **THE CHRISTIAN IDEAL OF LIFE AGAINST IRRELIGIOUS BOLSHEVISM**
>
> SOMEBODY said recently that the former articles about my experiences in Spain had not told people what they really wanted to know—was this in truth a war for religion.
>
> My own opinion is that it is a war for the defence of the Christian ideal of life against the irreligious ideal of Bolshevism. It is a war for the preservation of religious freedom, of the right of the in-

The battle for Irish public opinion continued with a clear divide between the two sides and proving yet again the old adage that 'in war, truth is the first casualty'. It would be fair to conclude that the vast majority of Irish support was in favour of the Franco side and in their belief that this was in defence of their Christian beliefs.

Last Words for Now

There were Irish men and women on both sides of the Spanish Civil War in terms of direct engagement, but also in terms of which side people were supporting. We will leave the last word for now to a report from late 1938 on a meeting of the Irish Friends of the Spanish Republic in Dublin. The Chairman, Mr Roddy Connolly, was arriving at a conclusion on the night when a member of the audience stood up and singled out the three main National newspapers for abuse accusing them of being 'the greatest curse of this country'. The Chairman supported the view in terms of the editorial policy of the papers in question, but, in what could be termed as a classic Irish response, exonerated the three journalists in attendance, as reported below.

The Irish Times Saturday 12th November 1938.[22]

> A member of the audience then turned towards the Press table, and, indicating the reporters, said: "And there you have the Trinity—the *Irish Times*, the *Independent* and the *Irish Press*—the greatest curse of this country."
>
> Mr. Roddy Connolly, who presided, then intervened, and said that, while they deplored the editorial policy of the papers in question, he hoped that none would attach blame to the three reporters present, who, he said, were "good trade unionists."

¡No pasarán!

Endnotes

1: *Irish Press*, 13 June. 1936.
2: *Irish Independent*, 20 July. 1936.
3: *Limerick Leader* 29 July. 1936.
4: *Irish Independent*, 4 August. 1936.
5: *Limerick Leader*, 26 September. 1936.
6: *Irish Times*, 23 September. 1936.
7: *Chicago Daily Tribune*, 14 November. 1936.
8: *Irish Independent*, 15 January. 1937.
9: *Irish Press*, 15 December. 1936.
10: *Irish Independent*, 15 December. 1936.
11: *Weekly Irish Times*, 26 September. 1936.
12: *Irish Independent*, 14 December. 1936.
13: *Irish Press*, 14 December. 1936.
14: *Irish Times*, 12 November. 1938.
15: *Irish Press*, 22 June. 1937.
16: *Irish Press*, 21 November. 1938.
17: *Irish Press*, 11 October. 1938.
18: *Irish Independent*, 20 December, 1938.
19: *Sunday Independent*, 11 December. 1938.
20: *Irish Times*, 16 September. 1936.
21: *Irish Independent*, 5 June. 1937.
22: *Irish Times*, 12 November. 1938.

Use of Images

My thanks to the Limerick Leader, Irish Times, Irish Independent, Sunday Independent and Irish Press for permission to use the images of reports in this article.

Flowers for Franco

A Curious offshoot in the Limerick Story

by Emma Gilleece

On the 28th of January 1939, the *Irish Press* reported that the Limerick Corporation congratulated General Francisco Franco on the capture of Barcelona aided by Fascist Italy and Nazi Germany 'on his fight for Christianity and freedom.' This laudatory gesture was accompanied by a bouquet of flowers for the Spanish dictator. Furthermore, this group passed a resolution demanding that the Fianna Fáil government 'recognise the Administration of the Patriot Leader' thus breaking diplomatic relations. The same government which unwaveringly stood by De Valera's declaration of neutrality in the face of immense criticism and pressure from the Allies during the Second World War. Limerick was the first Irish city and one of the first in the world to recognise Franco as the legitimate ruler of Spain. This event in the Limerick story is indicative of the Spanish Civil War's impact on Irish diplomatic policy and the intensity of Catholic religiosity in Ireland.

This short newspaper article stated that James Dalton proposed the resolution of congratulations, eventually seconded by Ald. James Reidy after Michael Hartney withdrew his secondment. Reidy took it further, requesting government recognition of Franco. The Mayor Ald. Dan Bourke responded to this request with 'We could leave that to the Government to decide.' Ald. Reidy's rejoinder defending the totalitarian dictator is today ironic with the benefit of hindsight 'We are free citizens of a free country and we are entitled to make a request to our Government.' In spite of Reidy's appeal, the Mayor was unyielding 'That is so, but we can be assured that our Government will do the right thing at the right time' and later would say 'We are only giving expression to the wishes of the people, irrespective of political views.' After receiving unanimous votes, Bourke finally declared both resolutions adopted, not because of the strength of Reidy's arguments but because his party did not control the corporation. This proposal to recognise Franco as the Spanish head of state by isolationist Éire came a month before both Britain and France.

> Limerick Corporation congratulated General Franco on the capture of Barcelona and on his fight for Christianity and freedom, and requested the Government to recognise the Administration of the Patriot Leader.
>
> Mr. J. Dalton proposed the resolution of congratulation, and when Mr. M. Hartney had seconded, Ald. J. Reidy said they should go a little further and request Government recognition of Franco.
>
> The Mayor (Ald. D. Bourke)—We could leave that to the Government to decide.
>
> Ald. Reidy—We are free citizens of a free country and we are entitled to make a request to our Government.
>
> The Mayor—That is so, but we can be assured that our Government will do the right thing at the right time.
>
> **AN AMENDMENT.**
>
> Mr. Dalton intimated that he would amend his resolution by asking the Government to recognise Franco.
>
> Mr. Hartney—Then I must withdraw from seconding you. This addition is calculated to embarrass the Government.
>
> Ald. Reidy—I will second the resolution. We are only giving expression to the wishes of the people, irrespective of political views.
>
> Mr. P. F. Quinlan having appealed for unanimity, the resolution was declared adopted.
>
> **SYMPATHY WITH THE JEWS.**
>
> On the motion of Mr. Hartney, a resolution was passed sympathising with the Jewish community on the persecutions.
>
> Mr. Dalton—We are only doing what our Holy Father has already done.

James Reidy and Michael Hartney would follow Dan Bourke in holding mayoral office, 1944-45 and 1945-46 respectively. Dan Bourke would be Mayor for a record period of five years. He joined the Volunteers in 1913 and was one of those who welcomed Pádraig Pearse, Éamon de Valera, Tom Clarke, Willie Pearse and other leaders to Limerick in 1915. He remained on the Republican side during the Civil War, was arrested in 1922 and imprisoned in Kilmainham and Mountjoy. The following year, he was transferred to Tintown No.1 Internment camp at the Curragh from where he escaped through a tunnel in April 1923. He was later recaptured and held prisoner for a considerable time. In 1920, he was elected a member of the Limerick Corporation in the Republican interest and was later to become one of the founder-members of Fianna Fáil.

Michael Hartney was also a Fianna Fáil member on City Council and was one of the most active members of the Volunteer movement during the War of Independence. His home in Davis Street was blown up by the Black and Tans as an act of reprisal. He was twice captured by the Black and Tans and served a term in Wormwood Scrubs Prison where he went on hunger strike. On his release, he resumed his volunteer activities and after being captured by the "Tans" for a second time, he was held as protection against I.R.A ambushes and was later interned on Spike Island. Hartney would be secretary for the Mid-Limerick Brigade of the Old I.R.A for over 40 years at the time of his death. As the exchange described in the initial report on the recognition of Franco government implied, Reidy was elected as a Fine Gael TD.

On the 25th of February, both the local and national press presented its readers with the extraordinary headline 'Franco's Thanks, Letter to the Mayor of Limerick.' Mayor Bourke had received the following letter from the National Government's Minister for Foreign Affairs, dated February 3rd;

> Dear Sir, On behalf of Generalissimino Franco, through his Minister for Foreign Affairs, I am to convey to you the lively gratification of his Excellency for the enthusiastic message of congratulations which you sent him on learning of the magnificent victory at Barcelona. I take this opportunity of extending to you my most friendly greetings.

Ironically, De Valera gave a statement to the Associated Press which appeared in newspapers only five days previously declaring '*the desire of the Irish people and the desire of the Irish government is to keep our nation out of war. The aim of Government policy is to maintain and to preserve our neutrality in the event of war.*' One can only imagine the reaction of readers in Limerick on the recording of this exchange between City Hall and Spain. One Dublin resident, a Mr R. Jacob, wrote an indignant letter addressed to the Mayor outlining his reaction to the news of the recognition of Franco 'This must be the greatest disgrace that ere has befallen the city of Limerick.' Mayor Bourke replied to this letter stating 'the resolution passed by the Limerick Corporation in regard to the victory of General Franco was an unanimous one, and he has, therefore, no apology to offer.'

This was not the first time that a fascist dictator involved in the Spanish Civil War had sent a communiqué to neutral Ireland. A telegram from Italy's Mussolini on the 13th of March 1937 contained a message of support for O'Duffy's Irish Brigade, which translates as '*Let the Legionnaires know that I am following hour after hour their action and it will be crowned by victory.*'

The recognition of Franco's regime, notwithstanding the fact that Reidy was able to convince his colleagues

---

FRANCO'S THANKS

LETTER TO THE MAYOR OF LIMERICK

In reply to a recent resolution passed by the Limerick Corporation, congratulating General Franco on his victory at Barcelona, the Mayor of Limerick (Ald. D. Bourke, T.D.) on Saturday received the following letter from the National Government's Minister for Foreign Affairs, dated February 3rd:—

Dear Sir,—On behalf of Generalissimo Franco, through his Minister for Foreign Affairs, I am to convey to you the lively gratification of his Excellency for the enthusiastic message of congratulations which you sent him on learning of the magnificent victory at Barcelona. I take this opportunity of extending to you my most friendly greetings.

The letter was written in Spanish and signed by the Foreign Minister.

of its validity, is not remarkable when taken within the overall social and political context. It must be remembered that the decades following the birth of the Irish State saw an unquestioning acceptance of clerical domination over education, health and public morality. This was particularly true in Limerick where the Arch-confraternity of the Holy Family attached to the Redemptorist Church of Mount St. Alphonsus had the highest level of attendance not only in Ireland but in Europe with 10,000 registered members in the 1930s. One contemporary commentator referred to Limerick as 'one of the most pious towns in Ireland.' The year 1936 saw the emergence of Patrick Belton's Irish Christian Front and general Irish opinion was overwhelmingly pro-Franco with O' Duffy's men leaving these shores to the sound of cheering crowds as they left to defend Catholicism. The war in Spain was seen as a religious rather than political conflict and Spain was regarded, like Ireland, as a historically Catholic nation. The nation took comfort in the fact that whatever divided Irish people politically, they were firmly united when it came to their Catholic faith.

The letter from the Corporation was not the only correspondence Franco received from Limerick that year. In July 1939, a Co. Limerick schoolboy, Timothy Ahern, wrote to the General congratulating him on his victory and expressed admiration of his 'great deeds in defence of Christian ideals.' The reply to this fan mail from Franco appeared in the local press in the September which read as follows:

> The Colonel Secretary of his Excellency, the Prime Minister and Commander-in-Chief of the National Army, salutes Timothy Ahern and he has the pleasure of presenting to him the thanks of the Commander-in-Chief for his congratulations on the victory of our glorious army, enclosing at the same time a photograph of the Commander-in-Chief in accordance with his desires.

In this age of social media sites, contemporary audiences have the benefit of up to the minute news reports and film footage. Armed with a smartphone, any ordinary bystander can have the capability of being a wartime correspondent. Before we judge the actions of these men in the council chambers in Limerick on that day in January 1939, we must bear in mind the exaggerated claims and propaganda they were fed. Franco fully appreciated the power of the media along with letters from Limerick.

FRANCO'S REPLY

TO CO. LIMERICK SCHOOLBOY

Last July a Co. Limerick schoolboy, Timothy Ahern, Laught, Lisnagry, wrote to General Franco congratulating him on his great victory and expressing admiration of his "great deeds in defence of Christian ideals." He has since received the following reply with a photograph of General Franco himself:—

"The Colonel Secretary of His Excellency, the Prime Minister and Commander-in-Chief of the National Army, salutes Timothy Ahern and he has the pleasure of presenting to him the thanks of the Commander-in-Chief for his congratulations on the victory of our glorious army, enclosing at the same time a photograph of the Commander-in-Chief in accordance with his desires.

"Francisco F.S.A. makes use of this occasion to offer you a testimony of his readiness to use his distinguished service."

Limerick and the Spanish Civil War

by Joe Malone

The burning of books is usually followed by the burning of people. This warning was given by Rosa Luxemburg, a woman well-acquainted with tyranny. She died in 1919; her death was due to a life-long struggle for intellectual freedom.

Her prophecy certainly came true in Spain. The burning of books by Franco was followed by the murder of people. García Lorca, who was the most popular poet in Spain, was murdered along with 4,000 Spanish intellectuals during The Spanish Civil War which was one of the bloodiest in modern history.

A fear of Communism on one side and a fear of Fascism on the other was one of the main causes of this horrible conflict. The Government forces under General Franco were responsible for the deaths of thousands of Basques. They murdered Basque priests and dumped them into holes without the last rites of their Church. They also showed no mercy to the lay population. Franco suggested to Pope Pius XI that the Basques should be condemned by the Vatican, but the Pope refused to do so. He was never very happy with Franco's relationship with Hitler and Mussolini. However, the Catholic Church in Spain backed the Generals in their revolt against a democratically-elected government.

By the middle of 1936, the war was being fully reported in Irish newspapers, but the reporting seemed to be very one-sided. The local papers for some unknown reason only saw the Franco side of the story. As far as the people of Limerick were concerned, nuns and priests were being murdered every day and priests began to preach from the pulpits about the rape of nuns and the burning of churches by the Reds in Spain.

A Limerick sailor arrived home from the port of Valencia, and gave a first- hand account of what he saw there. He told a local newspaper that he saw young men and women wielding guns openly in the streets. He also witnessed the burning of churches and this information added to the hysteria already being trumped up from platform and pulpit. A gut-wrenching sermon was given by Father Fox, the spiritual director of the men's confraternity, in which he praised the stand taken by the Limerick Trades Council who condemned the evils of the communists in Spain "even though they hadn't a bull's notion about the Spanish Civil War". Father Fox also said how proud he was "of the Catholic workers of Limerick, what a glorious catholic spirit they have displayed, what a great stand we have taken against Godless Russia".

"And today their Godless lips are licking Kerry Gold butter at a few pence a pound at the expense of the Irish."

Collections were taken up all over the city to help Franco and his soldiers. The press, clergy and politicians continued to talk about the atrocities being committed by the Reds in Spain. Most of what they said was true, with a slight bias here and there, but not one word of what Franco had done to the Basques. During all this ranting and raving from the pulpit and platform, Pope Pius XI, was receiving at the Vatican 600 Basque refugees, an act much detested by Franco and the Spanish Bishops. In October 1936, a meeting was held in the Town Hall, the mayor (Ald. Dan Bourke T.D.) presided. At this meeting Dan said: "Limerick would forever stand for the cause of Christianity. There was no great danger than Communism would come to Limerick".

The purpose of the meeting was to form a branch of the Irish Christian Front, the fanaticism and fervour was so rampant that Elmer Gantry or Paisley would sound tame. Limerick had made up its mind to fight the evils of Communism and from the meeting in the Town Hall a committee was elected, or should I say they elected themselves. The committee consisted of ex-blue shirts, ex-republicans and a fair number of clergymen. Some enlightened people expressed doubts about the true aims of the Front as they now became known.

A mass rally was held in Baker Place, bands from the City and County attended. The Corporation in their red robes prayed with the multitude, (I wonder what the Bard of Thomond would have said?). Dan Bourke T.D. "a freedom fighter in his day" denied the rumours going around about the real aims of the Front, which were considered by some of the Labour movement as being political. At the Baker Place meeting, Canon O'Dwyer, St. Munchins, said, now that they were going to aid their cousins the Spaniards to maintain their faith, "I foresee a day when an Irish Legion will lead the Spanish Army to Barcelona".

A proposal to maintain their loyalty to Christ the King was passed at the meeting, one speaker said "we are proud of our Christian ideals in this City". While this charade was going on an eviction was going on in the Island Field, now St. Mary's Park. Two families were evicted for not paying their rent, not a word was spoken in their defence, yet money could be found for the Spanish people.

The one-sided reporting continued in the local papers. Hysteria and jingoism was all these newspapers reported almost non stop, and now there was talk of an army going to Spain to fight for Franco. General O'Duffy was recruiting in different parts of the country.

In an attempt to explain the two sides of the Spanish Civil War, a Spanish priest came to Dublin where the Gaiety Theatre was put at his disposal, Father La Borda told his listeners about the Basque priests who were murdered by Franco's army, some of the priests were dumped into holes without even receiving the last rites of the Church. He also told the audience that Franco was a militarist. When he tried to explain the burning of churches which were being used as platforms for fascist propaganda, the people, he said, "feared Fascism as much as they feared Communism". At this meting, two Jesuits shouted him down. He met the same hostile attitude in the city of Belfast. In spite of this first hand knowledge from Father La Borda, the Irish people continued to support Franco. Hundreds of passports were issued by the Department of Foreign Affairs even though the Government stated that the War was an internal affair. 7,000 men volunteered to join O'Duffy who had more than a flair for private armies. He tried to start a small army during the building of the Shannon Scheme.

Fifty Limerick men volunteered to join O'Duffy's forces, some were from the city, some from the county. The final number chosen to go to Spain was 34. The guards were aware of the activities of the Limerick crusaders and they were on the lookout for troop movements. Some guards were positioned at the Railway Station, others were planted around the city, but the well organised O'Duffy troops gave the guards the slip. They left the city in motor cars and drove to Passage West. Before they boarded the ship they sang Faith of Our Fathers and the National Anthem. The ship that took the Irish Troops to Spain was German and was flying the Swastika. This was the same flag that flew over the German concentration camps where so many men, women and children would soon die horrible deaths.

When the Irish arrived in Spain, they discovered too late that they were wearing uniforms which were very similar to the Government Forces. Four of them got shot by Franco troops by mistake, four more died from food poisoning. The six hundred Irish voted to come home and some historians claim they never even fired a shot. The Irish, now demoralised, sailed for Ireland. Looking at the names of the Limerick men who went out to Spain, there is a noted absence of the politicians and clergy who encouraged these men to leave their homes to fight for Franco.

Written 1986
Limerick Property News

LOS BRIGADISTAS EN EL PALACIO DE DEPORTES 1997

'Hermanos, Madrid con vuestro nombre se agrada y se ilumino'
                                                Rafael Alberti

for Tom Enthwistle

Who failed to feel the chill of their courage
On our spines that night, the clenched fist
Of a more peaceful age, the glint of bravery
In our medallionless eyes – Living idols this side
Of a fifty-year-old Civil War grave.

Those men and women come home to Spain
To proudly claim their Pasionaria invitation;
Walk unforgettable outlines of battlegrounds
Where comrades fell; gave their young lives
To manure the olive fields with freedom.

Who among us did not tremble when history
Spoke and legend real as flesh, in voice recalled
Galapagar and Morata cemetery outside the wall –
Where the dumped remains of the Jarama dead
Were finally brought in for honourable rest.

And who if Irish failed to hear Wolfe Tone's plea
To 'abolish the memory of all past dissension';
Embrace the International names of those
Heroic examples of democracy whose presence
Stalked prosperity's indifferent streets,

Reduced noisy bars to silence, raised questions
In young minds about lost Republics,
The acceptable face of King Juan Carlos.
Those men and women of a more generous age
Who fought and died defending its citizens.

John Liddy

THE LIMERICK MEN

From the Shannon to the Ebro

Jim Woulfe *by David Convery*

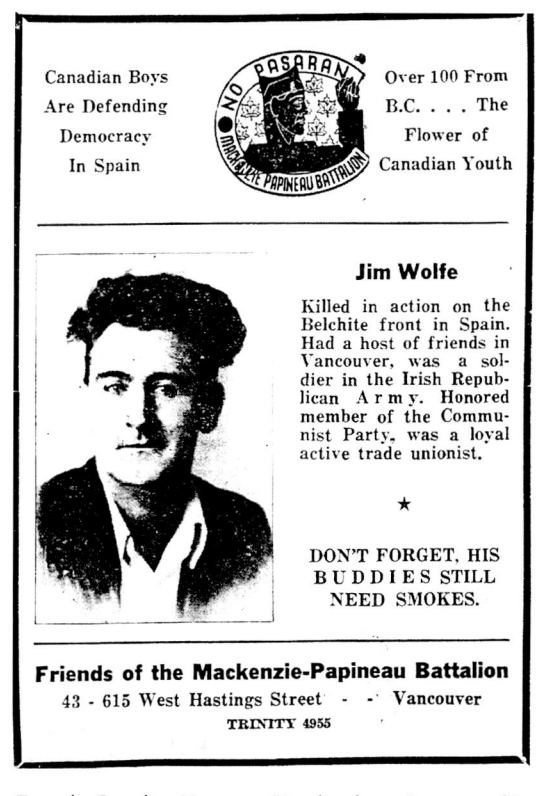

James Woulfe was born on 10 June 1899, and grew up in Athea, County Limerick. He was the fourth-born of seven children to Marryanne and John P, who worked as a draper and a farmer. In 1918, Jim joined the IRA and fought in the War of Independence and later the Civil War on the republican side following the Treaty split. However, he was captured by the Free State forces and spent from October 1922 to December 1923 in jail, whence he escaped to Canada, becoming a logger in British Columbia. Working-class life was harsh in Canada, and Jim became a union activist, joining the Communist Party of Canada in 1932. He became close friends with fellow logger, union activist and communist Pete Nielsen. Nielsen was a Dane, and had moved to Canada in 1916. 'Him and I stuck close together during the tough going in the years of '33-37. We roomed together in Vancouver and helped each other out when we were able to get a bit of work', recalled Nielsen. During the Great Depression, unemployment was rife and those who had work faced deteriorating conditions and pay. The Communist Party was to the forefront in organising workers in these years, but faced a clampdown from the state, and was temporarily declared illegal. One of its biggest campaigns at this time was organising outdoor relief workers, who worked for as little as twenty cents per day building roads and other infrastructural projects, into the Relief Camp Workers' Union. Their biggest event was the On-to-Ottawa Trek in 1935 which saw over one-thousand unemployed workers embark on a march east from Vancouver to Ottawa as part of a demand for better conditions; however, they made it only as far as Regina, Saskatchewan, before they were attacked by police. Many of Woulfe's comrades from the Communist Party and future fighters in Spain such as Nielsen, Ronald Liversedge, and Kerryman John 'Paddy' McElligott, were organisers for the march, and it is certainly possible that he was on it too.

From the Canadian Newspaper "Peoples advocate" courtesy of David Yorke

San Agustin Church, Belchite where Jim Woulfe was fatally injured.
Photo courtesy of Jaime Cinca

When the Spanish Civil War broke out in July 1936, it immediately caught the attention of the labour movement in Canada. Over the course of the war, almost 1,700 Canadians would join the fight to defend the Spanish Republic from Franco. Jim Woulfe was one of these, arriving in Spain in March or April 1937. At this time, the new arrivals from Canada joined the Lincoln or Washington Battalions, made up predominantly of volunteers from the United States. These were part of the mostly English-speaking XV International Brigade, which also comprised the British Battalion, and later, the nominally Canadian Mackenzie-Papineau Battalion. At the time of Woulfe's arrival, the Lincoln Battalion was engaged in action at the Jarama Front to the south of Madrid. At the beginning of July 1937, it, along with the new Washington Battalion, was sent into action with the rest of the XV Brigade as part of the Brunete offensive west of Madrid. I have not been able to find any evidence for Woulfe being engaged in action either at Jarama or Brunete, though it is possible he was there. The casualties from the Brunete offensive were so great that the two North American battalions merged to become the Lincoln-Washington Battalion. A roster places him, Private James Wolf [sic], as a member of Company No. 1 of the Lincoln-Washington Battalion on 14 August 1937.

At the end of that month, the 35th Division, including the XV International Brigade, was transferred to the bleak terrain of Aragón in the north-east of Spain with the aim of capturing Zaragoza and diverting attention from Franco's campaign in the north. The main fighting by the International Brigades took place in a number of towns near Zaragoza. It began on 24 August with the assault on Quinto involving the Lincoln-Washington Battalion. The Republican forces surrounded the town and then proceeded slowly by foot into the centre, under cover from tanks. The battle for the town was intense, involving dangerous street fighting and enemy sniper fire from the church tower. The Lincoln-Washington Battalion cut off the water supply to the enemy, and cleared buildings using improvised Molotov cocktails. When the town was captured after two days, the Lincoln-Washingtons were moved to take the nearby town of Belchite. As they approached it, they came under heavy sniper and machine-gun fire from the church tower, and immediately started taking heavy casualties. For six days they fought alongside the Dimitrov and a Spanish Battalion to take the town. All the company commanders and many of the adjutants were killed on the first day. The Lincolns were still coming under fire hundreds of metres from the town when they were ordered to take the church. This meant crossing open ground under heavy fire. In one assault, twenty-two men attacked and only two survived. However, the brigade commissar Steve Nelson found a culvert that led directly into the town, avoiding the need for a frontal assault.

Despite coming under heavy bombardment from the brigade's Anti-Tank Battery, the snipers still held out, and had to be dislodged from their positions through hand grenades and close-combat through individual houses. Street-fighting raged for days with the defenders falling back upon the thick walls of the church of San Agustín where they made their last stand. Two Irishmen, Charlie Regan, a veteran of the First World War, and Jim Woulfe, were killed. Woulfe's old friend from Vancouver, Pete Nielsen, recounted what happened:

> War seemed to completely stun him up till the attack on Quinto. There he appeared to have made up his mind to fight in the front ranks at every opportunity. During the attack on Belchite he was fatally wounded. He got it in the courtyard of the Belchite church when our unit was engaged in the first assault for possession of this stronghold. (September 3rd). A hand grenade exploded near his face smashing one side of the jaw and neck, also penetrating the opposite shoulder.
>
> He could not speak to me, but if it is permitted to repeat what his eyes said along with the complaint of physical agony, it would be: I lived – and I die for a better life for my class, and have no regrets. He could not smoke so he gave me his cigarettes.

Although hurt by his friend's death, it inspired him to go on. 'I tell you, it struck me pretty hard when Jim got it, but made me all the more determined to stay in Spain and go through with the whole thing (end of war).' Nielsen too would meet his end in Spain, reported missing in action, presumed killed, in March 1938.

I would like to thank Jim Carmody, David Yorke and Ciaran Crossey, who all provided information on Jim Woulfe.

BIBLIOGRAPHY

Files of the International Brigades held in RGASPI, Moscow, fond 545, op. 3, d. 469, l. 37 (Pete Nielsen's account) and an abridged version in:
Beeching, William, *Canadian Volunteers: Spain, 1936-1939* (Regina: Canadian Plains Research Center, 1989), p. 68
Other sources used in this piece include:
Carroll, Peter, *The Odyssey of the Abraham Lincoln Brigade: Americans in the Spanish Civil War* (Stanford: Stanford University Press, 1994)
Eby, Cecil D. *Comrades and Comrades: The Lincoln Battalion in the Spanish Civil War* (University Park, PA: The Pennsylvania State University Press, 2007)
Petrou, Michael, *Renegades: Canadians in the Spanish Civil War* (Vancouver: University of British Columbia Press, 2008)
Ryan, Frank (ed.), *The Book of the XV Brigade: Records of British, American, Canadian, and Irish Volunteers in the XV International Brigade in Spain 1936-1938* (3rd edition, Torfaen: Warren & Pell, 2003)

Joe Ryan
by Tom Collopy

In proud memory of Joseph (Joe) Ryan, (1916-1940), Volunteer, XV International Brigade
Spanish Republican Army, Brigade ID Number 406

When I was asked to write an article in Joe Ryan's memory, I was conscious of the fact that at various times in my own life, my father, Stephen. reminded me that "our past was the anchor to our future". It was with this in mind that I decided that Joe's extended family was the future he didn't live long enough to share and they are now the living reminders of his short life. Joe's extended family certainly merit mention in this effort to bring to life the embodiment of what moulded the thoughts of a young man to put his life on the line for a cause and a conflict that even by today's standards, took a lot of courage.

Joe's father, David Ryan, was born in Castleconnell Co. Limerick, in 1893. His mother died when David was still a child and he was raised in the CBS Orphanage, Roxborough Road, Limerick. This is indicated as his place of abode in the 1901 census, David was 9 years old. David's name again appears in the 1911 census, but his place of abode is now referred to as Main Street, Ennistymon Co. Clare. The reason for this change of address, looking at the details on the 1911 census form, is that he was an apprentice leather worker employed by Margaret Walsh, Ennistymon, and he was nineteen (19) at this time. David met Margaret Duhig of 4 Bank Place Limerick, and they married on the 5 October 1913 in the Church of St. Michaels in Limerick City. The Marriage Certificate indicates that Margaret's old address was their first home after the marriage. Margaret's father was Patrick Duhig, and he was a Cooper by trade. The couple had ten (10) children who were as follows: (Not necessarily in order)

Michael (Benny) Ryan:
Michael was a founding member of the Limerick and district angling club, and a former member of the Irish Republican Army (IRA).
May Ryan: *(Mc Fadden) lived in Kentish town UK all her life.*
Theresa Ryan: *(Ryan) Bourhamwood, England, married Hughie Ryan from Knocklong Co. Limerick*
Sarah Ryan: *(Bennett) lives at 28, Garryglass Ave, Ballinacurra Weston, Limerick.*

Joseph Ryan: *Former Spanish Civil War veteran and British Merchant Navy.*
Harry Ryan: *Harry had a fish and chip shop in Mungret Street, Limerick.*
Patrick (Paddy) Ryan: *A former paratrooper, he is buried in Mount St. Lawrence Cemetery, Limerick.*
Nancy Ryan: *(Hartnett)Bournhamwood, England*
Margaret Ryan: *(Treacy) of Sean Heuston Place, Limerick*
Eileen Ryan: *(Maloney) Lived in Ballynanty Beg, Limerick.*

Joe Ryan's father, David, had a business in Mungret Street selling footwear. Unfortunately, the vagaries of depressed times and the general economic situation resulted in the business going bankrupt, and he turned to shoe making and shoe repair. Within the family, it was said by Harry Ryan's wife Kitty, that the real reason the business went "bust" was because Mrs Ryan was "too soft" and took pity on people who could not afford to pay for footwear, with the predictable resultant closure. When the Ardnacrusha Power Station came on stream in 1929, David had this new-found miracle installed in his shop i.e. electricity, something of which he was very proud, and as he was a man who could read and write he would on a regular basis write and read letters for his neighbours and clients as the need arose.

The importance of family to this story, and the families of the other Brigadistas from Limerick, becomes all too evident when one considers the economic deprivations which again were sadly the norm in the Ireland that Joe and his siblings were born into. In an interview with one of my colleagues (Mike Mc Namara) a niece of Joe Ryan's, Dolores Brazil, spoke with pride of her possession of her war medals, and the specific instructions from her father, Michael, Joe's brother, to "never part with them".

Joe Ryan was the second child in a family of ten (10), four boys and six girls. As a young boy, he attended the Christian Brothers School (CBS), Sexton Street Limerick. His older brother, Michael (Benny) joined Na Fianna Éireann (Republican Boy Scouts) in 1926. Later, Michael became an active member of the Irish Republican Army

Family believes that Joe Ryan is person in middle of back row. Seen here with comrades injured at Jarama. Frank Ryan back right.

(IRA), and served time in both Arbour Hill Prison and the Curragh detention camp for his political activities.

Young Joe left Limerick between his sixteenth and seventeenth birthdays. He initially lived at Parade Street, Edgware Road, London. It is not clear as to when Joe became politically aware, but there are indications that he looked up to his older brother and his path on the road to political activity was probably formed before he left for England. Soon after he had settled in London, he joined the British Labour Party, and the Transport and General Workers Union; his occupation was listed as Labourer. When Franco rebelled against the elected Republican government in Spain, Joe, like many of his colleagues, volunteered their services and departed for Spain to fight for the Republican cause.

Joe Ryan arrived in Spain in December 1936 just in time for the coming fight that became known subsequently as the Battle of Jarama. Like most of the Brigade members he, in all probability, received very rudimentary military training before being assigned to the 15th International Brigade in early 1937. It is important at this juncture to contrast the trench warfare scenario of the Spanish Civil War with that of the combatants in the trenches of the First World War. On average, men in the trenches of WW1 fought, ate, and slept for up to three and four weeks in the trenches before being sent to rear areas for rest and recreation (R & R). In the Spanish Civil War, this form of trench warfare meant that because of the lack of Republican reserves, it was sometimes 60 and 90 days before being relieved from what was in effect a war of absolute attrition. This is relevant later on in the story of Joe Ryan. It would appear that Joe was either wounded or injured to some extent, because he is listed as such in a field hospital in Albacete on the 26 June 1937. In the photograph above Joe has been identified by family members as the man wearing the beret; to his right is Frank Ryan. As a result of the conditions experienced by some of the volunteers, it was not unusual for men to sometimes "wander" from their positions to get some succour from the constant bombardment from the Nationalist positions.

In that context, there is one particular incident which occurred at approx 15.00 hrs on the 12 May 1937. Both Joe and a Brigade colleague named Joseph Moran (originally from London) were found to have

HMS Dunvegan Castle

entered the port area in Valencia without the relevant documentation. Two security officers attached to the Commissary arrested them. They gave their names and indicated that they were members of the 15th International Brigade. There was an attempt by the Area Commissar to interrogate the two men but according to the "documents of detention" the officer on duty (D. Obrial Valesco Acero) prevented this as there was an issue with language without the benefit of an interpreter. The badly-interpreted charge sheet indicates that both men were then handed over to an officer of the International Column with a copy of the proceedings detailing the reasons for their detention. It was not long after this incident that Joe was identified as having TB, and was repatriated, through the British Consul, back to the UK.

At the outbreak of the Second World War, Joe joined the Merchant Marines seeing this as his opportunity to continue his fight against fascism. Joe was assigned to the armed merchant cruiser HMS Dunvegan Castle. At this time, German u-boat activity was particularly active in the North Atlantic. The following information was gleaned from the log book of U46, of the 7th U-boat flotilla. It was commanded by Captain Englebert Endrass, who took command of the U Boat in May 1940. U46 departed from its base in Kiel on the 1 June 1940, and headed for the North Atlantic, returning on the 1st July. In one month the U46 sank the following vessels:

Carinthia	(Auxiliary Cruiser)
Margarita	(Finnish ship)
Athelprince	(8782 tons)
Hymettus	(Greek ship)
Barbara Marie	(British Merchantman)
Willow Bank	(British Merchantman)

Having restocked in Kiel, U46 again departed for the North Atlantic, having first had a stopover of four days in the port of Bergen, Norway. Soon thereafter, the U boat sank the Alcinous (Dutch), and the L. Valvas (Greek), which was so badly damaged that it was towed to port and scrapped. It was also responsible for an unsuccessful attack on the HMS Hood during that period.

I give this information to the reader to give some indication of the day-to-day dangers of plying merchant vessels in the North Atlantic at this juncture in the war.

On the 27 August, the U46 was "cruising" off the west coast of Ireland, and, as stated by Captain Endrass, it was relatively quiet only being disturbed by two "alarm dives" when allied aircraft were spotted during the course of the day. He ordered a change of course to the "hunting grounds" off the North west coast of Ireland. There, at 19.00 hours, he spotted the HMS Dunvegan Castle, all 15,007 tons of her. The HMS Dunvegan Castle was launched on the 26 March 1936. She was requisitioned in September 1939, and converted by Harland and Wolff to an armed Cruiser. This was now the vessel that Joe Ryan was serving on as a Fireman.

At approximately 21.47 that night, Captain Endrass ordered the firing of a single torpedo from a distance of 400 yards which struck the Cruiser at the quarterdeck. The Dunvegan Castle continued its course, at which stage Captain Endrass ordered another torpedo to be fired at the stricken ship, but dived when he thought the cruiser was about to return fire. He surfaced again 10 minutes later, and fired the second shot, this time hitting the engine room. After coming under fire from the Dunvegan Castle, the U boat dived for approximately 30 minutes. When it resurfaced it fired the third and final round, this time hitting the forward quarterdeck. It was at this stage that the cruiser began to burn, and "list "significantly. Captain Endrass noted in the log, and I quote, "Not even the best built steamers can survive three hits and a fire on board, and remain floating. The Dunvegan Castle remained afloat all that night, but sank the following morning with the loss of four Officers, and 23 Ratings, one of whom was Fireman Joe Ryan of Limerick City Rep. of Ireland. The survivors were picked up by HMS ships, Primrose and Harvester.

Joe Ryan, volunteer in the 15th International Brigade, survived his participation in the Spanish Civil War only to lose his life still fighting fascism on board the Dunvegan Castle on that memorable night of the 28 August 1941, resolute, no doubt, to the end.

Note
Oberstleutnant Englebert Endrass was awarded the Knights cross soon after the sinking of the Dunvegan Castle and continued as the commander of the U46 until September 1941, when he was transferred to U567. He was killed in action two months later on the 21 of December 1941 when U567 was sunk off the Azores with the loss of all 47 of its crew.

Tony Bennett, Joe's nephew, was very helpful with regard to family records for the extended Ryan siblings, and for that, I and the Memorial Trust are grateful.

Liverpool Naval Memorial

Gerard Doyle *by Mike McNamara*

Gerard Bonaventure Doyle was born on the thirteenth October 1907 at number 25 Island road Limerick.[1] His father, Peter, was a cattle dealer who came from 88 High Road in Thomondgate and his mother, Elizabeth (Lizzie) O'Connor, came from the Island Road area of Limerick where her brother Patrick had a small farm holding. According to the 1901 census, Lizzie's twin brother, John, was a brass moulder by trade and her brother, Francis, was a cabinet maker.[2] Peter and Lizzie were married in or about 1903 and their first child, Francis, was born in Liverpool in 1904 and they had a daughter, Mary, born about 1906[3] (it is believed that she died sometime in 1920). By the time of the 1911 census, the family lived at No. 36 Upper William Street Limerick where they operated a lodging house.[4]

Gerard went to school at the nearby Christian Brothers School on Sexton Street .[5] Alice Barrett remembered Gerard Doyle since they were both kids; she came from the Waller's Well area of Roxborough and was attending the Presentation Convent girls' school also on Sexton Street. According to Alice, the Doyles had a water tap in their yard at their premises in Upper William Street which had public access; she used to go there to fill bottles of drinking water. She maintained that Gerard was her boyfriend at that time, even though they were only about 12 years of age then. In an interview with Des Ryan, Limerick historian, in February 1999 (when Alice was almost 90 years old), she fondly recalled her early days at school and said that she had never forgotten her first love - Gerard Doyle.[6]

Ireland in the 1920's was a place of great turmoil, a country divided by wars and conflict, political campaigning and industrial unrest. The legacy of the War of Independence and the Irish Civil War was economic deprivation. Housing was poor in Limerick and living conditions were hard; all this activity was going on while Catholic religious dominance was on the rise and Limerick was no different to any other part of the country during these troubled times. It was against this background that Gerard Doyle left school in 1923 to serve his apprenticeship as a moulder at the Harrison Lee's City foundry. Later that year, in October 1923, Gerard's mother, Lizzie, died aged just 39 years.[7]

Drawing of Gerard Doyle (sketch by Clive Branson)

It was while working at these premises in 1926 that Gerard along with his co-workers went on strike due to the fact that the company tried to enforce a 25% reduction in pay.[8] The Limerick Leader of 27th February 1926 reported at Page 5 - CITY STRIKE FOUNDRY WORKERS OUT. The fitters, moulders, smiths and smiths' helpers employed at the Shannon and City Foundries, Limerick struck work to-day. The employers, it appears, decided on a reduction of wages by 25 per cent, and to this the men objected and 'downed tools' this morning. The number of workers affected is about thirty".

After about six weeks on strike, the management of the Shannon Foundry accepted the unanimous decision of the Limerick Conciliation Board that there be no cut to the employees' wages, however the strike at Harrison Lee's foundry continued.[9] In July 1926, the workers were laid off and Richard A. O'Neill of 93 O'Connell Street, Limerick, was appointed Receiver to the company, as a result of which the company was offered for sale by Private Treaty as a going concern.[10]

Finally, in December that year, after 96 years of continuous service in Limerick City, the great engineering and foundry firm of Harrison, Lee and Sons came to an end as all hopes of re-starting the factory were abandoned after months of trying to sell the factory as a going concern failed to attract a satisfactory offer.[11] The machinery was dismantled and offered for sale as separate lots with the site finally being sold for the building of housing.

By this time, Gerard left home after his father had re-married and he spent approximately twelve months working with his Uncle Patrick (his mother's brother) at the farm on the Island road. During this time, he soon realised that he was being used by his uncle as a means of cheap labour and decided to part ways in pursuit of suitable employment. In 1927, Gerard found employment on the Shannon Scheme at Ardnacrusha, Co Clare, not far from Limerick, where he worked as a Loco-driver and Fireman. Work on the Government scheme on the construction of the Hydro Electrical plant was well under way and upwards of 3,500 men were employed by the German firm, Siemens, who were the main contractors engaged on the project.[12]

However, he was once again to find problems at work. The Germans were a very tough employer and they forced both skilled and unskilled workers into working 12 and 14 hours per day for ordinary rates and no

A group of workers from Harrison Lee and Sons, the old city foundry, c.1900, from the most recent edition of the Old Limerick Journal. The photo was donated to the Limerick city museum

Harrison Lee's City Foundry

overtime. Speaking at the Irish Labour Party and Trade Union Congress that year, Mr. E. P. Harte (Transport and General Workers Union) described the conditions which he asserted existed on the Shannon Scheme at Ardnacrusha:

> We have a colony of Germans who use the most vile epithets in the German and English languages to the workers employed there, and they do not stop at that – they use the fist and boot on the Irish workers. I was no particular friend of the British Empire during the war, yet I think that many of the people who prayed for the success of the German arms must now regard it as a good job that they did not succeed and rule this Country.

Mr. L J Larkin (Limerick Trades Council) in response said:

> Mr Harte made his statement in all good faith, but the skilled tradesmen of Limerick had not closed their eyes to the position of the un-skilled workers on the Shannon Scheme. The three unions involved, the Amalgamated Society of Woodworkers, the Engineering Unions and the Labour Party had done everything possible to maintain recognised union conditions. [13]

Railroad at Ardnacrusha

Nonetheless, work on the Shannon Scheme was to be completed by 1929 and the German paymasters would not let the unions slow their progress. Three new bridges were to be constructed at O'Brien's Bridge, Clonlara and Blackwater and new stores were to be constructed at Donnellan's Field and Long Pavement, to replace stores damaged by fire some months previous. In the first week of December 1927, the first stone on the foundations of the great dam was laid by the German Engineer, Mr. Weye. The stone sourced for the dam was granite from the quarries at Aughrim and, by now, many stone masons and stone cutters were employed on the scheme bringing a much-needed boost to the local guild members.[14]

Work on the scheme progressed steadily, however, and as 1929 dawned, the *Limerick Leader* reports were very worrying, "Gloomy Outlook -Trade Depression in Limerick" the headlines screamed. Upwards of 3,000 workers were unemployed; more workers were added to the list on an almost daily basis; the Bacon factories had seen a decided slump since the passing of the Christmas trade resulting in 150 workers being released; the building trade which was at one time brisk was reportedly stationary with numerous masons and other workers now idle; the flour trade was anything but flourishing and the Limerick Docks had shown a major decline in business. Due to the lack of continuous orders, many casual workers at the Limerick Clothing Factory had been laid off.

Fifty men had received their notice from the Limerick Loco works, adding to the distressed conditions of the city. Owing to the introduction of a new transport system by Messrs. Guinness, the employment of a number of lorry drivers and other workers had been discontinued. Limerick County Council, it is reported, dismissed a great batch of road workers, and rumours were abounding that large numbers of workers were about to be discharged from the Shannon Scheme where, up to now, this was the only employer absorbing large numbers of unemployed.[15]

However, unlike the process of repetitive factory productions, every day spent working on a construction site meant a day nearer to your dismissal as when the project is completed there will no longer be employment for the construction workers at that employment, and so by September 1929, the newspapers were reporting the dis-employment of the overwhelming majority of the Irish workers on the Shannon Scheme and the return home to Germany for the greater number of German engineers and mechanics and their wives who had set up colony at Ardnacrusha, Co Clare.[16] Gerard Doyle was one of the thousands of Irish workers who lost their jobs in the autumn of 1929, and with no prospects of work in the city's economically-depressed industries, Gerard left his native city and travelled to Cork in search of much-needed employment.

Ford Motor Company Cork

When Henry Ford launched their Model T Ford motor car, they could not have foreseen the success of the car that brought motoring to the masses, and introduced motoring on a scale never before seen. By this time, the company was manufacturing cars in twenty countries worldwide. There had been a decline in business at the Cork Marina facility due to the imposition of tariffs by the British Government on imported car parts which were being exported to the Ford Company production factory in Manchester. This was reciprocated by the Irish Free State Government which meant that the Ford Company experienced additional operational costs which altered the economics of the Cork plant so much so that it divided it from the major European customer base.

Ford was by now the only major manufacturing company in both Britain and Ireland, and because of the hostilities between both countries resulting from the legacy of the War of Independence and the Civil War, the company was attracting tariffs in both directions. An earlier introduction of tariffs by the then Chancellor of the Exchequer in Britain, Reginald McKenna, in May 1915 had been doubled over the course of the following years and in the case of luxury goods a 33.33% tariff was applied. Luxury goods included cars, car parts, cycles, watches, clocks and musical instruments. However, tractors were not described as luxury goods and were exempt from the higher charges. The company decided to invest its sole worldwide tractor manufacturing business at the Cork facility and predicted that by 1st January 1929 the Cork Marina facility would be a self-contained and self-supporting profitable plant for the production of the "Fordson" tractor. Ultimately, the change from production of car parts for export to Britain to the manufacture of the Fordson tractor for export worldwide brought with it a boom in the motor industry in Cork.

So, not long after Gerard Doyle arrived in Cork in late 1929, he found work at the ever- expanding Henry Ford Marina factory in Cork where the company had just recently reinstated tractor production which quickly went on to become the company's sole tractor facility and global supplier of Ford tractors. The number of workers employed at the Cork facility rose from 1,327 including manual workers and inspectors in January 1929 to a total of 6,712 in February 1930. However, in a reversal of their good fortune, the economic depression hit hard after the Wall Street Crash in the United States on 24th October 1929, spreading out from America and collapsing like a house of cards across Europe. The American Congress reacting to the economic depression at home introduced the Smoot-Hawley bill which proposed to impose a high tariff against all imports into the United States. On the 17th June 1930, the Smoot-Hawley bill became law and, almost immediately, the Cork Ford factory hit the headlines again announcing up to 6,000 layoffs citing a slight downturn after a six month period of sustained activity. Gerard Doyle was once again among the ranks of the unemployed.[17]

Being out of work in an economically-depressed country which was trying to rise out of the depths of worldwide depression, the prospects of finding alternative employment was greatly diminished, so Gerard Doyle joined the Irish Free State Army. He was engaged in the Mechanical Transport section as a driver. The Transport Corps was responsible for the procurement, management and maintenance of all vehicles within the Defence Forces and also for the provision of heavy lift equipment for the army. Having completed one full term, Gerard refused to sign on again and left the army.[18]

In 1934, having left the army, Gerard had vast experience of driving heavy vehicles and, as a consequence, he had no problem securing employment driving the buses in Dublin. At that time, there were many private bus companies operating in a de-regulated transport industry. The government policy, however, was to eliminate competition on the railways and in the road transport business and to encourage the transfer of business to the three main statutory transport companies set up under various pieces of legislation, namely, the GSR, Great Southern Railway; GNR, Great Northern Railway and the DUTC, Dublin United Tramway's Company, and to give them a monopoly in the transport industry.

While introducing the Road Transport Act, 1932, the then Minister for Industry and Commerce, Mr. McGilligan, told the Dáil that the tendency in the Act was "to divert traffic into the hands of the three transport companies operating on a big scale at present". The number of companies operating in the country rose from 96 in 1928 to 145 in 1932, prior to the commencement of the Road Transport Act.[19] As a result of this act being passed, the number of independent bus operators started to decline and eventually by 1935 with the amalgamation of the independent contractors almost complete, Gerard Doyle was once again at the receiving end of Government legislation which was to cost him his job and so, in July of 1935, he was let go after almost 15 months of driving the buses in Dublin. After a few months of idleness and finding it was almost impossible for him to get another job, he left for England to search for work.[20]

In January 1936, Gerard Doyle arrived in England and while he soon got work at his own trade, that of a moulder, the pay was very bad, so he moved from job to job in search of better conditions. The money he earned was only barely enough to eke out an existence. It was while working under such primitive conditions that

Dublin bus 1930s style

Gerard's social conscience was awakened and he joined the Communist Party in Birmingham in 1936, which ultimately led to his departure for Spain to help in the fight to crush the rising fascism.[21]

Gerard Doyle arrived in Spain in early 1937, and it is speculated that he joined the XVth International Brigade at the Madrigueras centre where up to 600 men, both veterans and new recruits who had arrived from England, Scotland and Ireland, left for the Jarama Front where they engaged in what was to become one of the most famous battles of the Spanish Civil War. Thousands of men lost their lives here in the Valley of Jarama as they desperately tried to prevent the encirclement of Madrid, fighting to keep the road to Valencia open from the fascist onslaught whose troops included the Spanish foreign legion and infantry and Moroccan Regulares from the Army of Africa. They were supported by German troops from the Condor Legion including two heavy machine gun battalions and a tank corps.[22]

In July 1937, the newly-promoted Sergeant Doyle found himself involved in fierce fighting at Brunete, 15 miles west of Madrid where the battalion had been sent to support the Republican offensive organised to relieve pressure on Basque forces fighting in the North. Under the control of General Miaja, the army was well equipped with over 136 pieces of artillery, 128 tanks and 150 aircraft. Their task was to attempt to cut off the Nationalist forces outside the capital, Madrid. Ger Doyle was injured at Brunete and spent a number of months out of action recuperating. The new year found him again in action in the Battle of Teruel, one of the bloodiest of the war, and, by March as the brigade was desperately fighting in a rearguard action in what is now called the great retreats in Aragon, he was captured by

Campo de Concentracíon, San Pedro de Cardeña.

Italian troops at Calaceite near Gandesa on the Ebro Front. He was imprisoned along with Frank Ryan at the brutal concentration camp, San Pedro de Cardeña. [23] *The Irish Times* of August 16th 1938 reported that Gerald Doyle, of Vale Road, Forest Gate, London, was among the prisoners still held at San Pedro, and also reported that Major Frank Ryan was among the other Irish prisoners held there.[24]

On the 25th October 1938, Gerard Doyle was repatriated back to England with Hugh O'Donnell. Under the headline "Freed By Franco" the *Limerick Leader* of 27th October 1938 reported "Two bronzed Irishmen – Hugh O'Donnell, of Burtonport, Co Donegal and Gerald (sic) Doyle, of Upper William Street Limerick were among the forty men from these Islands taken prisoner by General Franco's forces and released from concentration camps under the exchange of prisoners agreement who arrived at Victoria from Hendaye."[25] Meanwhile, the *Irish Independent* was reporting that Doyle who spent 22 months in Spain and who had been captured near Gandesa on the Ebro Front was among forty men, including three from Ireland, who had been released by General Franco and who had arrived at Newhaven in Sussex.[26]

After the war, Gerard Doyle returned to live in England where he worked as a factory boiler stoker. On the 2nd August 1950, aged 43 years, he married Violet Annis Louise Weeks, a 47 year old spinster. They were married at the Registry Office in Brighton and both were residing at No. 24 Mount Street at the time. The Marriage Certificate shows that Gerard's father was Peter Doyle, a cattle dealer, and that Violet's father, Harry Weeks, was deceased and had been a factory timekeeper.[27]

On the 10th April 1953, Gerard's father, Peter, died at his residence at No. 2 St. Munchin's Terrace, Thomondgate, Limerick, aged 74 years.[28] Peter was buried at the family grave in Mount St Lawrence Cemetery Limerick where his wife, Lizzie, son, Richard and daughter, Mary (Maureen) were also buried.[29] Gerard Doyle died at the Lamellion Hospital, Liskeard in Cornwall on the nineteenth of March 1970, his next of kin was listed as Francis James Doyle, his brother. This is the same person who was shown in the 1911 Irish census as being the eldest son of Peter and Lizzie Doyle and who had been born in Liverpool.[30] Gerard is laid to rest at Liskeard St Martins's Churchyard which adjoins the church of St Martin's in Liskeard in the Diocese of Truro. He is in grave number 22 in the newest part of the churchyard along by the hedgerow, in an unmarked grave.[31] In May 1970, just two months after the death of Gerard, his wife Violet, Annis Louise Weeks died in the Chanctonbury district of Sussex in England, aged 68 years.[32]

In his own words, in his autobiography, Gerard Doyle gave his reason for going to Spain:

There and then I got the Idea into my head that it was only a waste of time working for what you got. That while Capitalism and Fascism reigned supreme the workers would be their slaves. There and then I abandoned all hopes of seeing anything good, until fascism is crushed.[33]

BIBLIOGRAPHY

1 Gerard Doyle's birth certificate, civil registration number 701217
2 1901 Irish Census Returns for Limerick
3 1911 Irish Census Returns for Limerick
4 Ibid
5 Gerard Doyle Autobiography from the Moscow Files
6 Alice (Barrett) Conlon interview with Des Ryan in Limerick 09/02/1999
7 Mount St Lawrence Burial Register Limerick Oct 10th 1923 D 75
8 Gerard Doyle Autobiography from the Moscow Files
9 Limerick Leader 17/05/1926 page 3 "Limerick Foundry Workers"
10 Limerick Leader 31/07/1926 page 4 "Iron Foundry and Engineering Works For Sale"
11 Limerick Leader 13/12/1926 page 3 "Loss To Limerick"
12 Gerard Doyle Autobiography from the Moscow Files
13 The Irish Independent 03/08/1927 page 10 "Shannon Scheme Workers"
14 Limerick Leader 17/12/1927 page 7 The Shannon "Front"
15 Limerick Leader 23/09/1929 page 3 "A Gloomy Outlook"
16 Limerick Leader 07/01/1929 page 6 "Things That Matter"
17 Gerard Doyle Autobiography from the Moscow Files
18 Gerard Doyle Autobiography from the Moscow Files
19 BUS DEREGULATION IN IRELAND Sean D. Barrett FTCD Trinity College Dublin
20 Gerard Doyle Autobiography from the Moscow Files
21 Gerard Doyle Autobiography from the Moscow Files
22 No Pasaran The story of the Irish volunteers who served in the International Brigades in the Spanish Republic against International Fascism 1936-1939
23 Ibid
24 Irish Times 16th August 1938 page 7 "Franco's Irish Prisoners"
25 Limerick Leader 27th October 1938
26 Irish Independent 27th October 1938 page 14 "Irishmen In Contingent"
27 Certificate of Marriage, Brighton registration no MXG 094033
28 Limerick Leader 11th April 1953 page 14 "Deaths"
29 Mount Saint Lawrence Burial Records – Jim Kemmy Municipal Museum Limerick
30 Certified copy of Death Certificate for Gerard Doyle issued at Liskeard in the County of Cornwall reference number QBDZ 202043
31 Email from Elaine McNamara amateur historian Welbury North Yorkshire England on 12th January 2014
32 Death Register in Chanctonbury, Sussex England for April, May and June 1970
33 Gerard Doyle Autobiography from the Moscow Files

Emmett Ryan
by Alan Warren

Family of Emmett Ryan (Emmett is centre front row)

Maurice Emmett Ryan was born on 6th May 1915 at 41 Catherine Street, Limerick. He was the fourth of six sons born to Edward and Mary Ryan and was known as Emmett to his family. His mother, Mary Cusack, was born and reared on a farm at Ballysimon on the edge of the city. His father, Edward, is also thought to have come from East Limerick. They were married in June 1910 in St. Patrick's Church Limerick, by which stage Edward lived in the former George's Street, now O'Connell Street, and his occupation was stated as Clerk.

Over the next ten years, they lived at various addresses including John's Villas and Alphonsus Avenue before acquiring the "41 Bar" in Catherine Street in 1914. During that period, they had six sons in quick succession; John in 1911,Thomas in 1912, Edward in 1913, Maurice Edward in 1915, Michael Kevin in 1916 and Oliver Plunkett Desmond in 1919. They were obviously quite enterprising and over the next number of years they acquired 40 Catherine Street and developed a Hotel on the site which they called "The Desmond Arms". This, they ran successfully until they disposed of it at auction in 1929. Little is known of their subsequent whereabouts, but in 1941, the family was living in comfortable suburbia in Rush, Co.Dublin where Emmett's mother, Mary, was a successful Kerry Blue breeder and his father worked as a furniture dealer.

What is clear is that Emmett came from a prosperous, conservative Catholic family. One brother Des (Oliver Plunkett Desmond) played rugby for Leinster and Ireland and Kevin (Michael Kevin) played for Munster. He was educated by the Jesuit Order at Crescent College and is reputed to have possessed a wild streak. In the early to mid 1930s, with financial support from his family, he was living in Lisbon, Portugal, where he ran foul of the authorities and was arrested and fined for being drunk and disorderly. In 1937, Emmett worked for a short period as a Steward aboard the "Empress of Australia", a well-appointed cruise ship which sailed between Southampton and Quebec in Canada.

It is not clear why Emmett enlisted with the International Brigades. He came from a conservative background and he claimed that at least one of his brothers had enlisted with O' Duffy to fight with the Nationalist forces in Spain. His demonstrated excellence as a machine-gunner suggested that he may have had some prior training in this area, He was a tall imposing figure, standing well over 6 feet tall and certainly did not conform to or fit the profile of the typical Brigader in that he seemed to treat the whole affair as an adventure and perhaps was not as committed politically as others. He had a fondness for the local wine and that may have been a significant contributory factor in his subsequent downfall.

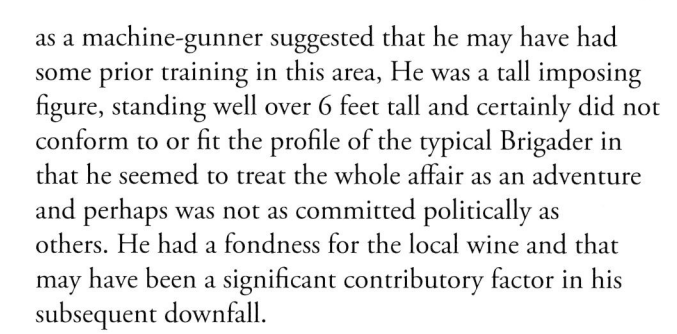

Emmett entered Spain in November 1937 having enlisted in Paris with the International Brigades. He was involved in a number of drink-related incidents including insubordination shown to officers and rowing with policemen, and was regarded suspiciously by some of his superiors for his somewhat diffident approach to the whole affair. Nevertheless, he fought bravely and suffered a shoulder wound at Teruel on 24th or 25th January 1938, He crossed the Ebro River with the XV International Brigade on the 29th July 1938 and his battalion made rapid progress towards their objective, the town of Gandesa. However, enemy reinforcements with sustained artillery fire and aerial bombardment halted their progress. Numerous attempts to capture the heavily fortified "Hill-481" overlooking Gandesa proved to be fruitless and costly, with many casualties. The battalion withdrew on August 3rd. Emmett died having been executed by his own battalion.

Emmett Ryan is just one of the many enigmas of the Spanish Civil War. He is one of at least three members of the British Battalion known to have been executed during the war. From the wealth of material available on the individuals who served in the British Battalion of the XV International Brigade, four accounts stand out; John Dunlop, Jim Brewer, Eugene Downing and Tom Murray. They all confirm the execution of Emmett, but not the exact date. It is likely that he was executed on either the 31st July or the 1st August. The circumstances of his tragic death at the hands of his comrades deserve greater study as there is some evidence to suggest that he did not deserve such a fate.

There is no doubt he was a popular man in the battalion but was no respecter of rank, often challenging the "comic tars" as he cynically referred to the Commissars. However, he was a very good machine gunner. On the occasion of Pandit Nehru's visit to the battalion at Marca, while the all-Spanish maxim gun crew were overawed by the occasion, Emmett proceeded to demonstrate his skill and bravado by grabbing the gun from them and knocked chunks out of a tree across the valley. Mention is also made of a competition at Marca on the occasion of the British Battalion's fiesta on July 18th 1938, which involved Emmett:

> Most of the competitions had been finished. All except one which continued with increasing intensity. It was between two heavy machine gun crews. One led by Bennett and the other by "Paddy" Ryan. Captain Fletcher backed Ryan and Sam Wild backed G. Bennett. The contest was to run the gun into action, mount the barrel on the carriage, load it, sight the target and pretend to fire the first shot. This carried on long after the games were more or less over. Feelings were high and there was plenty to drink. A crowd had gathered round. Suddenly, it happened.

Gentleman abroad

The gun was in position, loaded, target sighted and the trigger pulled. The silence was broken by an exploding cartridge. A young Spaniard cried out and sank to the ground. Those near to him rushed to help. But it was too late. He was already dead. That was the end of the July 4th (sic.July18th) Celebrations in Marsa (sic). This did not improve relations between the English and Spanish. They refused to let any English attend the funeral. (Jackson, 2008: 101)

There is no evidence to suggest which of the gun crews was responsible for the death of the young Spaniard or, if indeed, they were responsible at all. George Wheeler in his account of the event described it as follows:

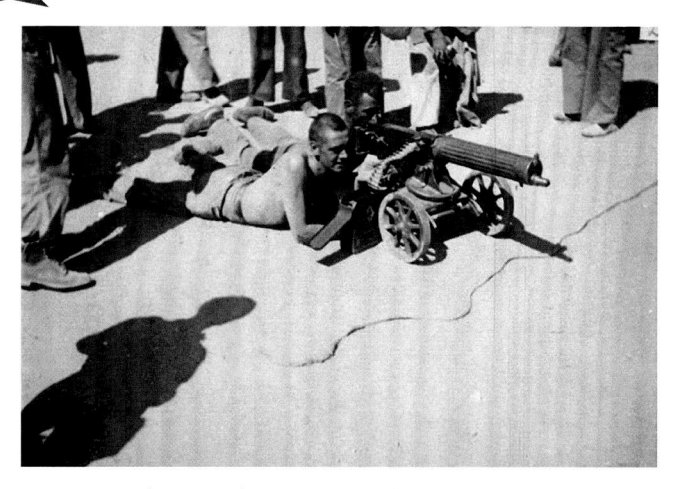

Emmett (seen here on right) manning machine gun.

Seated and relaxed, we settled down, many hundreds of us in the afternoon sun, to watch the main attraction of the fiesta: the machine gun competition. This was conducted in heats in which two crews at a time competed. Each crew had to run with their gun to a given spot and assemble, load and fire at a target and then unload. All went well and the competition was played out with great enthusiasm. When the winners were announced, men surged on to the field, crowding around the guns, all interest and curiosity. Someone pressed a trigger. There was a report, a groan and three men were wounded-one seriously. He was a young Spaniard and had been hit in the stomach. It was a pitiful sight as he lay there calling for his mother while the first-aid men cut away his clothing and tried to staunch the flow of blood. I sensed that life was slowly ebbing away from him, and indeed he died on the way to hospital. (Wheeler, 2003:59-60)

So why was Emmett executed? He was accused of firing on his own comrades at the Ebro and was reportedly summarily executed by his Commanding Officer, Sam Wild, and his Adjutant, George Fletcher. There is no doubt that he was incorrigible and liable to bouts of drunkenness and was not popular with some sections because of his cavalier approach. His command of languages, good looks, perceived bourgeoisie upbringing and lifestyle prior to enlisting niggled many of his working-class comrades. However, there is some evidence to suggest that the equipment he had was perhaps faulty and there were no casualties resulting from his wild firing or that he was on the machine gun at all at that time. There is a case to be made that he should have been sent to a labour battalion where the risk of death was very great, instead of being executed. He was a young man of 22 years and perhaps did not deserve such a fate, yet this was war. The same conditions that affected the regular soldier, poorly- armed and fed, under enormous strain from constant frontline service for long periods, and the impending defeat of the Republic, also affected the equally-young officers. His inclusion on the battalion Role of Honour and the letter sent to his mother telling of his death "at the hands of a fascist execution squad" would reveal a certain regret as to how he died.

Perhaps the final observation should be left to his friend and fellow Irish Brigader, Eugene Downing:

He was a bit of a problem in the battalion. He was a larger than life character. He was from Limerick and according to himself had been to university in England. He was a tall, burly person, a complete extrovert and fearless. He was also an excellent machine gunner. On the occasion of Pandit Nehru's visit to the battalion at Marca he demonstrated his skill with that weapon knocking chunks out of a tree across the valley. He could be a very amiable and amusing character. Unfortunately, he was always kicking against the pricks, in a manner of speaking.

On one occasion, when I was on sentry duty at battalion headquarters he was placed in my care until the following morning on a charge of being drunk and abusive. He just lay on the ground and went asleep. The following morning he used his charm and powers of persuasion to induce me, when I was going off duty, to fetch his mess tin when I returned to the camp and bring it back to him. To me this was above and beyond the call of duty, but he succeeded in getting me to do it.

MID-SOUTH MEMORIES

Warning signs

STAFF PHOTO

City Court Judge Carl Stokes (left) was on hand Nov. 6, 1950, to see the first of 100 traffic safety signs being attached to a Memphis Street Railway coach. The signs show a traffic judge warning "Speeders Always Lose." Col. Roane Waring, transit firm president (center) and Tom O'Ryan study the warning. The signs were donated by Tom O'Ryan Advertising Agency and will be seen on coaches and buses until Jan. 1, 1951.

pileup

YALONDA M. JAMES/THE COMMERCIAL APPEAL

...est Memphis on Wednesday. Two drivers were killed and ... of the interstate for more than four hours.

dead, 4 injured

...ed when officials allowed the first vehicles in the miles-long backup to proceed. Westbound lanes coming from Memphis were largely unaffected.

Shelby County jail staff indicted

■ Military leave misuse alleged by four jailers

By Samantha Bryson
s.bryson@commercialappeal.com
901-529-2339
and Clay Bailey
bailey@commercialappeal.com
901-529-2393

Four deputy jailers with the Shelby County Sheriff's Office were indicted on charges stemming from an internal investigation of employee absences and misuse of military leave, Sheriff Bill Oldham said Wednesday.

Among the four people charged were three current deputy jailers and one former deputy jailer. Sheriff's officials identified them as Stephen Vaughn, 32; Sedric Ward, 46; and Alvin Williams, 24, who are still with the SCSO, and Josette Whorton, 45, who resigned from the sheriff's office in October 2012. All face charges of theft between $1,000 and $10,000.

The three current employees are suspended without pay pending a disciplinary hearing, said Chip Washington, spokesman for the sheriff's office. The trio were given an opportunity

Vino was his downfall. During the Ebro battle he turned his gun on his own comrades while roaring drunk. Eventually he was executed. All this was well known to those of us in Mataro Hospital as new casualties arrived during the battle. I heard additional details from Prendergast in London during WW2. Sam Wild had given him the details. Sam and George Fletcher had taken Ryan for a walk and informed him of the decision that had been taken. He responded calmly; 'You wouldn't do that Sam would you?' But he was wrong. He was shot in the back of the head.

I was always sceptical about the rumours that he was a spy. It is not the custom of spies to go around waving banners, shouting the odds and generally drawing attention to themselves. Since he was aware that we were preparing to cross the Ebro it seems remarkable that Franco was taken by surprise.

Some Spy!

With many thanks to Jim Carmody, Richard Baxell, Barry McLoughlin and especially to Ger McCloskey of the Limerick International Brigades Memorial Trust and also the countless friends and colleagues who helped me in exploring the lives and experiences of the men and women who served in the International Brigades. A special "thank you" to Maurice Emmett Ryan's nephews, Michael and Eamon Ryan, and niece, Mary Davis, for the photographs and previously unknown information on their uncle.

Des and Kevin Ryan, noted rugby players in their day.

Porta de la Historia.

BIBLIOGRAPHY

Crossey, Ciaran (ed.). I*reland and the Spanish Civil War.* Eugene Downing, 1913-2003. A collection of articles by this veteran of the Spanish Civil War. n.d. Pamphlet 7, International Brigade Commemoration Committee, Belfast.

Jackson, Angela, *At the Margins of Mayhem. Prologue and Epilogue to the Last Great Battle of the. Spanish Civil War"* Warren & Pell, Abersychan. 2008.

MacDougall, Ian, (ed.). *Voices from the Spanish Civil War.* Polygon, Edinburgh. 1986

Wheeler, George, *To Make the People Smile Again.* Zymurgy Publishing, Newcaste upon Tyne, 2003.

Wolff, Milton, *Another Hill ("an autobiographical novel").* University of Illinois Press, 1994

Paddy Brady *by Danny Payne*

Patrick Joseph (Paddy) Brady (International Brigade ID No. 123) was born in 1905 in New Road, Thomondgate, to James and Agnes Brady. Paddy had four sisters and one brother and attended the local St. Munchin's Christian Brothers Primary School. Upon leaving school, he, like his father, worked as a bootmaker. He is reported to have been engaged in the Civil War and in the War of Independence, but information on this period of his life is scant. He subsequently left for England.

New Road Thomondgate
Photo courtesy of Sean Curtin, Limerick - A Stroll Down Memory Lane
Photographer: Michael Cowhey

Time in Liverpool

Patrick Joseph Brady on arrival in Liverpool settled in the crowded working-class neighbourhood just off Brownlow Hill. The area is to be found contained within a triangle made up of the Adelphi Hotel, constructed to service the rich Transatlantic passengers travelling to and fro from America on the Cunard Liners, the Grand Victorian Arches of Lime Street Station and the large Municipal Work House, now the site of Liverpool's Metropolitan Catholic Cathedral. Patrick lived at No 43 Trowbridge Street with his wife Mary, herself born in Liverpool to a family of Irish descent and their five children. The working-class population of the city depended largely on casual work on the Docks or in warehouses clustered around the water front. The work was hard and intermittent in the late 1920s and through most of the 1930s as a result of the Wall Street Crash and the Coalition Government policy of austerity. Lives that were hard became harder still. Patrick supplemented this casual work with his skills as a shoe maker and repairer. At the time of writing, there are still people of an older generation who remember taking their families' shoes to Patrick for repair.

He was politically active in both the Communist party and in the NUWM (The National Unemployed Workers Movement) having been on several demonstrations and marches in protest at the living conditions for ordinary working families at the mercy of the bosses. Poor housing and education provision and rudimentary health care were provided largely through charity. The battle for a welfare state in Britain had yet to be won. The protests of Liverpool activists like Paddy also focused on the dreaded and despised PAC (public assistance committee). The panel was made up of the Great and Good of the Merchant class that ran Liverpool as a safe Tory Town -the city made safe for the Conservative interests through dividing the working class with the old chestnut of sectarianism - a state of affairs that allowed Liverpool remain a Tory stronghold for much longer than other northern industrial towns. When work was thin on the ground, the poor had to appear before this committee, cap in hand, and beg for assistance. The committee would make a decision as to whether they were the "deserving or undeserving poor" and assistance would

March at Birkenhead demanding an end to non-intervention

be given or not. The relief received was barely enough to survive on.

Paddy and those like him on the Left in Liverpool and in the larger area of Merseyside also fought with the local representatives of Sir Oswald Mosley's British Union of Fascists, over who offered a message of hope for ordinary working people in desperate times.

Mosley visited Liverpool in October 1936, a few months before Paddy and many of his mates on the left went to Spain. An estimated 10,000 people crowded around the Adelphi Hotel where Mosley was staying and also on the plateau of St Georges Hall in front of Lime Street Station. The men and women of Liverpool showed their true colours on that day and put their sectarian differences aside and gave Mosley and the Tory City Police the fright of their lives as the ensuing pitched battle turned into a series of running battles through the city centre. It should be no surprise then that of those arrested and later charged, two-thirds of them would soon be on the way to Spain to fight fascism or be the relatives of those who would go to Spain.

Spain and Spanish Civil War Period

Paddy's daughter, Mary, told of how he had told his wife he was going on a Hunger March with the NUWM, and that he would be gone for maybe a week. Some days later, someone called at the house to inform the family he had volunteered for Spain.

Paddy crossed over into Spain before the hypocritical and one-sided (in favour of Franco) non-intervention pact came into effect. Unlike later volunteers who had to climb over the Pyrenees in the dead of night to escape the attention of the non-intervention patrols, Paddy went before the border was closed and probably crossed by coach.

He and those with him made the long slow journey first to Barcelona and then by train south to Albacete and joined the "British Battalion" on 07/ 01/ 1937 which meant he received a month's training before seeing action. This training was, in some cases, pretty basic, and due to the shortage of arms because of non-intervention, some of the boys only got to fire two or three rounds of ammunition through a rifle before the lads in the Battalion were flung into the furnace of battle at Jarama. It appears that Paddy was fortunate to come out of Jarama unscathed, unlike so many of the other Liverpool and Merseyside lads. At least 18 men from the Liverpool area met their end at Jarama and although the number of wounded is not known, it can be estimated to be 3 or 4 times that of those killed. Only Glasgow, as a city, lost more good men on the Jarama battle field.

It was at the Battalion's next Battle at Brunete that his luck ran out while approaching a village across the wide coverless 15 square kilometre plateau that encompassed the Brunete battlefield. The Battalion's approach to the fortified villages was out in the open and under the gaze of the fascists installed in the village church tower. From here, they rained down machine gun and sniper fire on the approaching International Brigade. One of those snipers' bullets smashed into Paddy's shoulder. We have no surviving account of the painful and long journey he made from the battlefield to hospital and then repatriation to Liverpool in November 1937. We know, from the accounts of others, that although the medical services of the Republican forces had improved, the care and treatment was, at times, basic as supplies of medical aid struggled to get through the blockade on Republican Spain.

Paddy and daughter, Mary.

Food for Spain campaign - Paddy seen her third from left handling food aid parcel.

After Spain, Second World War and after

The family at home had heard nothing from Paddy and knew nothing of his fate until his young daughter, Mary, playing in the street when down Trowbridge Street walks "Daddy" with his arm and shoulder encased in a plaster cast. She ran into the house shouting to her mother that Daddy was home. Apparently, Paddy just popped his head around the door said he was home and was just off to the pub.

The late great Jack Jones, later General Secretary of the TGWU and himself a volunteer in the International Brigades, mentioned that Paddy and other returning volunteers, some wounded as he was, helped collect food aid for the starving people of the strangled Spanish Republic. They collected enough food and supplies from those sympathetic to the cause in Liverpool and the surrounding area to fill a ship and Paddy and others volunteered once more to load it.

The Spanish Aid committee provided support for the family until he was able to work again. Work, once difficult to come by, was now readily available as a new World War loomed. There was no money for the deprived area of Britain under the coalition's austerity plan but with Empire under threat, money was now found and work was available for everyone. However, dangerous communists like Paddy were kept away from sensitive work on the Docks. Also, those who tried to enlist to fight the fascists once again, found it difficult. Their experience fighting German, Italian and Spanish Fascists and Nazis was seemingly not wanted. After 1941, this changed and Paddy was called up to serve.

After the war, men like Paddy had their cards marked, and blacklisting was in place for activists like him. As a result, many of them struggled to find employment in the new industries in the post-war period. His daughter, Mary, said that being working class in Liverpool made things hard. Being Irish and a socialist made it even harder.

Frank Ryan *by Manus O'Riordan*

The Limerick Republican Fighter for Freedom in Ireland and Spain

The Irish-language inscription on Frank Ryan's tombstone in Dublin's Glasnevin Cemetery reads:

Proinnsias Ó Riain. Frank Ryan. Rugadh in Elton Conndae Luimnighe 1902. D'éag sa Dresden 1944. Tugadh a chorp thar nais dá thír dúthcais 22-6-1979. Do throid sé ar son na saoirse sa tír seo agus sa Spáinn. Go dtuga Dia luach a shaothair dó. A cháirde agus a ghaolta a thóg an leach seo.

The wooden cross placed on his earlier grave in Dresden's Loschwitz cemetery by his close friend, Mrs. Elizabeth 'Budge' Clissmann (née Mulcahy), had simply read:

R.I.P. J Francis Richard. Proinnsias O Riain. 11.9.1902-10.6.1944.

70 years ago, on 10 June 1944, Frank Ryan, the Limerick-born leader of the Irish International Brigade volunteers who fought in the Spanish Anti-Fascist War, died at the relatively early age of 41 years and 9 months. His funeral was arranged by Budge Clissmann and he was buried in Dresden, Germany on 12 June 1944. 35 years later, which is also 35 years ago, Frank Ryan's remains were repatriated from Dresden to his native land by his Irish International Brigade comrades-in-arms – Frank Edwards, Peter O'Connor and Micheál O'Riordan – for reburial in Dublin's Glasnevin Cemetery on 22 June 1979.

Author delivers graveside oration in commemoration of Frank Ryan at Glasnevin Cemetry 2005.

But, what a story is hidden behind those few Irish-language words on his tombstone! A freedom fighter in Ireland and Spain; yet death in Nazi Germany, having lived there under the pseudonym of J Francis Richard! No wonder that the first biographical study of Ryan by his fellow Limerick man Michael McInerney was entitled ***The Enigma of Frank Ryan***. Part One of that study was published by the late great Limerick Socialist, Jim Kemmy, in the December 1979 issue of *The Old Limerick Journal*. Irish International Brigade veterans, Peter O'Connor and Micheál O'Riordan, in recognition of Kemmy's commitment to honouring the heroes of the Spanish Anti-Fascist War, travelled to Limerick in September 1997 in order to give him a Connolly Column salute at his funeral. Kemmy also published Part Two of McInerney's study in the March 1980 issue of *The Old Limerick Journal*, but McInerney had sadly passed away in January 1980, so that what initially had been intended as a dry run for a full biography never came to fruition.

In the same year of 1980, however, came the definitive biography authored by Seán Cronin, simply entitled ***Frank Ryan: The Search for The Republic***. That it was such a definitive biography was due not only to the fact that Cronin had been given access to such a treasure trove of both information and insights that were to be found in the wartime correspondence between Ryan in Berlin and de Valera's Minister in Madrid, Leopold H. Kerney – with all of Ryan's letters being reproduced in full as appendices to the book – but also due to the

Frank Ryan seen here addressing a public meeting in 1932. Courtesy: National Libary of Ireland

supreme integrity of Cronin himself in leaving not a stone unturned in telling the whole story of Ryan's life exactly as he found it, and leaving it to the readers to draw their own conclusions.

But what of the next biography of Ryan? Fearghal McGarry had first made his mark as a historian with a pioneering work entitled **Irish Politics and the Spanish Civil War** (1999), described by me as "the definitive textbook on the subject" in the Fall 2003 issue of Irish Literary Supplement, a Boston review of Irish books. This was in the context of a review of his second book, entitled **Frank Ryan** (2002), a slight biography which I criticised as both disappointing and sensationalist with little evidence of the depth of research and analysis required in order to do justice to its subject. The hope was nonetheless expressed that the author's future work would demonstrate a return to the "high standards of scholarship, balanced presentation and conscientious evaluation" that he had previously shown. This, McGarry certainly achieved in his next biography,

Eoin O'Duffy – A Self-Made Hero (2005), which I favourably reviewed in the Spring 2006 issue of I*rish Literary Supplement*. But McGarry's biography of Ryan will always stand to his discredit. A further biography by Adrian Hoare entitled **In Green and Red: The Lives of Frank Ryan** (2004) was an honourable volume of work that complemented Cronin with the integration of recently released British intelligence files in the objective manner that had been eschewed by McGarry. Finally, Fearghal McGarry went on to be the historical advisor for Desmond Bell's feature film, The Enigma of Frank Ryan (2012), which title had, of course, been borrowed from Michael McInerney's original *Old Limerick Journal* article.

Frank Ryan was born in Elton, Co. Limerick, on 11 September 1902, the son of a schoolteacher. While attending St. Colman's College in Fermoy, Co. Cork in 1920, he became a member of a local IRA battalion which would have brought him into contact with the IRA's outstanding North Cork Brigade commander,

Seán Moylan. A quarter of a century later, when my father, Micheál O'Riordan was the Cork Socialist Party candidate in the 1946 Cork by-election and was denounced by the Fianna Fáil Minister for Local Government, Seán MacEntee for having been an International Brigade volunteer who had fought against Franco in Spain, the Fianna Fáil Minister for Lands, Seán Moylan, made a point of distancing himself from MacEntee by crossing the floor of the count centre to shake hands with my father and share reminiscences of Frank Ryan.

Ryan had been serving with the IRA's East Limerick Brigade at the time of the War of Independence Truce in July 1921. He opposed the Treaty, rejoined the East Limerick Brigade, was wounded in action and interned by the Free State, but later released in November 1923. In 1926, Ryan became Adjutant of the IRA's Dublin Brigade and he took over from Peadar O'Donnell as editor of the IRA weekly *An Phoblacht* in 1929. Ryan was once again imprisoned by the Free State Government in January 1932, but released by the newly-elected Fianna Fáil Government in March 1932. In the meantime, under the influence of George Gilmore and Peadar O'Donnell, he was becoming more and more socially conscious and moving leftwards. By 1933, Ryan had quit *An Phoblacht* and, breaking with the IRA along with Gilmore and O'Donnell, he co-founded the Republican Congress in 1934.

A fierce opponent of Eoin O'Duffy's fascist Blueshirts, Ryan's initial response to the Franco revolt against the Spanish Republic in July 1936 was to declare his support for that Republic but also argue that for Irish Republicans the battle lines were in Ireland itself. When, however, Eoin O'Duffy set off for Spain with an Irish Brigade in support of Franco's fascists, this changed situation was to call for a radical re-assessment on Ryan's part. In December 1936, Frank Ryan himself led a contingent of Irish Anti-Fascists to fight in defence of the Spanish Republic. Ryan was a gifted leader of men. At the battle of Jarama in February 1937, when Franco's military offensive attempted to break the road from Madrid to Valencia, it was Ryan's inspiring leadership, before he himself was wounded, that managed to reverse a rout of Republican forces when he led International Brigaders in mass singing of the "Internationale" as a war song that spurred them on to retake lost ground. Ryan and his fellow brigadistas thus ensured that the link between the two cities was never broken. Small wonder that Ryan was chosen by the International Brigade Commissariat of War to edit ***The Book of the XV Brigade: Records of British, American, Canadian, and Irish Volunteers in the XV International Brigade in Spain 1936-1938.*** It was at Calaceite on the Aragon Front that Frank Ryan would be taken prisoner by Italian Fascist troops on 31 March 1938. Notwithstanding that it placed him in greater danger of summary execution, Ryan insisted on identifying himself as an officer of the Spanish Republican Army. A German Gestapo officer asked Ryan why was he in Spain and not in Ireland fighting the British. Ryan stated that it was the same fight, and asked the Gestapo officer what it was that **he** was doing in Spain. He, in turn, replied that Ryan was a brave man. Captured along with Ryan were Waterford International Brigader Jackie Lemon and Dublin International Brigaders, Maurice Levitas from the South Circular Road Jewish "little Jerusalem" neighbourhood, and Bob Doyle from the Northside inner city. Bob Doyle was to relate to me that, as the Republican prisoners were being marched away by their fascist captors, Frank Ryan remarked to Bob: "They published my book today." Some book launch!

Frank Ryan was initially imprisoned along with Jackie Lemon, Maurice Levitas and Bob Doyle in the notorious San Pedro de Cardeña concentration camp, but on 12 June 1938, he was removed to Burgos Prison to face capital charges and – with the active encouragement of Sir Robert Hodgson, the British representative at Franco's court – was sentenced to death. The Ryan family believed that it was the personal intervention and representations made by de Valera that ensured commutation of that death sentence. Dev's Minister in Spain, the veteran Republican diplomat, Leopold Kerney,

Banners calling for release of Frank Ryan from the prison camp of San Pedro de Cardeña

was scrupulous in visiting Ryan in prison and making representations on behalf of his welfare. Kerney also bore witness to Ryan's departure from Burgos for Germany on 14 July 1940.

On 16 October 2005, I gave the oration at Frank Ryan's grave on behalf of the International Brigade Memorial Trust on the occasion of the last such commemoration to be attended by his fellow brigadistas – Bob Doyle, Jack Jones and my father, Micheál O'Riordan. During the course of that oration, I stated:

> When the Irish International Brigade poet, Charlie Donnelly, was killed in the battle of Jarama in February 1937, two unpublished poems were found among his personal effects. The first, entitled "The Tolerance of Crows" was published a year later by Frank Ryan in ***The Book of the Fifteenth Brigade***. The second, which was simply entitled "Poem", had been inspired by the integrity of their mutual friend, Republican Congress leader, George Gilmore. This Charlie Donnelly poem has much to say to us as to the challenge of setting the record straight, not least in respect of the life of Frank Ryan himself.

The major part of "Poem" has Donnelly's character assessment of the test that he himself would ultimately face – and courageously pass – as well as his tribute to Gilmore and how the latter might be remembered:

Between rebellion as a private study and the public
Defiance, is simple action only on which will flickers
Catlike, for spring. Whether at nerve-roots is secret
Iron, there's no diviner can tell, only the
moment can show.
Simple and unclear moment, on a morning
utterly different
And under circumstances different from what you'd
expected.

Your flag is public over granite. Gulls fly above it.
Whatever the issue of the battle is, your memory
Is public, for them to pull awry with crooked hands,
Moist eyes. And village reputations will be built on
Inaccurate accounts of your campaign. You're name
for orators,
Figure stone-struck beneath damp Dublin sky.

Micheál O'Riordan, father of Author, in his International Brigade uniform.

I further observed:
> Having his memory pulled awry, as anticipated in Charlie Donnelly's poem in respect of George Gilmore, is indeed a long-standing experience in the case of Frank Ryan. In June 1958, *The Irish Times* published a sensationalist denunciation of Ryan by the former second-in-command of the Third Reich's Abwehr Intelligence agency, Erwin Lahousen, in which he pilloried Ryan as 'the Irish Communist', 'a wild Irishman … of a distinctly Red complexion', 'a ruffian' and 'nothing but a gangster'. And, in October 2005, it was again *The Irish Times* that published the sneering reference by the Newfoundland academic historian Peter Hart ('famous/infamous' for his character assassination of Tom Barry, based on a thoroughly fictitious account of the November 1920 Kilmichael ambush – MO'R) to '*Frank Ryan, the Republican saint/Nazi collaborator*'.

Frank Ryan was none of these things. A life-long Catholic, he was, in fact, a James Connolly Republican Socialist. His Republicanism was that of Wolfe Tone, with the objective of uniting Catholic, Protestant and Dissenter under the common name of Irishman. He denounced Catholic sectarianism no less than he did Protestant sectarianism. Frank warned against the development in Ireland of any sympathy for what he called the 'disease' and 'plague' of Hitlerism, and he specifically denounced any anti-Semitic hostility towards Dublin's Jewish community. Frank Ryan's internationalist solidarity with the Spanish Republic was also of a kind that brought together volunteers from all over Ireland, both North and South, and from the best of the Catholic, Protestant and Jewish working-class traditions in this island. He proclaimed that he was fighting against fascism in Spain in order to prevent its triumph in Ireland. And there was none braver in that good fight.

Following his brutal incarceration by Spanish Fascism for over two years, Frank's life was to be saved in July 1940 by the combined efforts of the Irish Minister to Spain, Leopold Kerney, and two members of Abwehr intelligence in Germany, Jupp Hoven and Helmut Clissmann, who, as former members of a left-wing National Bolshevist organisation – the Young Prussion League – had formed a friendship with Ryan on visiting Ireland a decade previously. And this action to save Frank's life was sanctioned by none other than the Taoiseach, Eamon de Valera himself.

Frank Ryan and Helmut Clissmann 1941
Courtesy: Seán Cronin's "Frank Ryan"

There are, however, those ever-prepared to traduce Ryan's character in respect of the final four years of his life spent in Germany. The slander can be summed up in one word "Collaborator", the title of that chapter in the 2002 biography of Ryan by Queen's University academic Fearghal McGarry, historical consultant to the 2012 movie entitled *The Enigma of Frank Ryan*. In the May-June 2012 issue of *History Ireland*, I became the unnamed target of a complaint by Des Bell and Fearghal McGarry in their article entitled "The Enigma of Frank Ryan" – the same title as that of their film. Their complaint was that "before the first scene of *The Enigma of Frank Ryan* had been shot, our film had been denounced by an *Irish Democrat* article headlined 'Film to slander Frank Ryan as Nazi Collaborator'. They did not name the author of the offending article and were being unfair to that publication on two counts. All it had done was reprint my posting on the Abraham Lincoln Brigade Archives website, and all I had done was respond to a *Sunday Times* report of film-maker Des Bell's own declared intention. "Queen's set for Nazi Occupation" was the heading in the Irish edition of *The Sunday Times* on 11 September 2011 when reporting that Queen's University Belfast had been festooned with Nazi insignia to represent wartime Berlin for a film being made by Desmond Bell of that same university, entitled *The Enigma of Frank Ryan*. The report quoted Bell on the declared purpose of the film: **'What we are really trying to do is to present to the audience the kind of enigma that Frank Ryan was – how he started out on the left and ended up working for fascism.'** The film's historical consultant was stated to be fellow Queen's academic Fearghal McGarry, author of **Frank Ryan** (2002), with one character assassinating chapter headed: **'Collaborator, 1938-44'**.

The completed film was premiered at the Jameson Dublin International Film Festival on 18 February 2012. The publicity material generated for its marketing contained the same message. "Wartime Berlin comes to Queen's" was the proud boast of the press release from Queen's University itself, which continued "Academic and film-maker, Professor Des Bell and historian Dr Fearghal McGarry, both from Queen's, are taking on one of their biggest assignments to date with the production of a film on the enigma that was Frank Ryan. Ryan, born in Limerick in 1902, was a teenage IRA volunteer, irregular in the Civil War, dissident republican socialist of 1930s Dublin and International Brigade volunteer who fought fascism in the Spanish Civil War, **and ended his life working for the Nazis in wartime Berlin.**"

Drawing of Frank Ryan by fellow-prisoner in Burgos, Goico Aguirre. Courtesy: Seán Cronin's "Frank Ryan"

While, under the heading of "The ex-IRA man who died a Nazi collaborator" in the *Irish Examiner* on February 16, 2012, one Richard Fitzpatrick sounded off "**Frank Ryan fought in the Irish and Spanish Civil Wars but became a Hitler stooge. A new film tells his story.**"

The film received a second showing on 26 February 2012 followed by a 'Hedge School' debate organised by *History Ireland* in which I participated. While not disavowing the character assassination still continuing to be deployed in the promotion of his film, Bell's screenplay had actually pulled back from some of the excesses of the "collaborator" line that, however, continues to be championed by McGarry himself. Indeed, I am less happy with some of the film's caricatures of 1930s Irish Republican controversies and of Ryan in the Spanish Civil War – riddled with many inaccuracies – than of its portrayal of Ryan in Germany. At the *History Ireland* 'Hedge School' I welcomed the fact that it had retreated from its previously stated purpose and now presented the complexity of Ryan's position in Germany.

In that *History Ireland* debate, Fearghal McGarry did, however, return to the '*collaborator*' thesis that he had advanced in his 2002 biography of Ryan, while I, in turn, restated the '*patriot*' argument of my review of that book for the Spring 2003 issue of *History Ireland*. The Oxford English Dictionary has a very precise political definition of '*collaborate*' as '*cooperate traitorously with an enemy*', while Oxford's Thesaurus further defines '*wartime collaborator*' as '*sympathiser, traitor, quisling, fifth columnist*'. By no stretch of the imagination can any of those terms be applied to Ryan. In an interview with Michael McInerney of *The Irish Times* in April 1975, de Valera's own judgement was that '*Frank Ryan was a man for whom I have always held the highest regard. In all he did at home or abroad he had as his first aim, the interests of his own country.*'

The *History Ireland* 'Hedge School' was the first occasion McGarry was willing to debate his decade-old Ryan thesis with me. In that debate, I welcomed the fact that the film had retreated from what its advance publicity had originally said it was setting out to do, namely, "show how Ryan ended up working for fascism". The film did indeed deal with the complexity of Ryan's period in Germany, even if not sufficiently so. I added that I was particularly pleased by the very honest depiction of the Irish Minister to Spain, Leopold Kerney. I pointed out that this represented a welcome rehabilitation of a patriot diplomat who had been made the victim of repeated character assassination by an Irish academic establishment far too heavily influenced by the libels penned by T Desmond Williams who had been made professor of History at University College Dublin following his acknowledged service in the ranks of British intelligence. Although the film had retreated from the Fearghal McGarry charge that Ryan was one of Nazi Germany's Irish collaborators, he himself, nonetheless, stuck to that hobby horse of his in responding to my opening remarks at this 'Hedge School' debate. While acknowledging that Ryan "was clearly not a willing collaborator in any ideological sense", McGarry, nonetheless, argued that "Kerney, when he is debriefed back in Dublin in 1941, said that Ryan returned to Germany to engage in some kind of *collaboration*; strangely enough, he uses the word collaborate." However, McGarry's fellow-panellist, David O'Donoghue, sought to establish some linguistic difference with McGarry: "I am sort of reluctant to get into an argy-bargy and point the finger; I am very reluctant to point the finger and say: Frank Ryan, oh yes, Nazi Collaborator! I think that would be a gross oversimplification." But then, O'Donoghue proceeded to once more regurgitate Francis Stuart's 'Quisling' slander of Ryan. I argued that the only term one could use to describe someone like Frank Ryan – who was defending his own country's interests – was *patriot*. I added that it was only from a Stalinist or Churchillian perspective on the Second World War that one could ever use the term collaborator to describe Frank Ryan.

David O'Donoghue was being shamelessly disingenuous in that debate. In his most recent book, **The Devil's Deal: The IRA, Nazi Germany and the Double Life of Jim Donovan** (2010), he regurgitated the following fantasy: "If, indeed, (the Nazi German agent) Gőrtz had planned to install a 'quisling' Taoiseach in Dublin, it is tempting to speculate on the possible candidates. The IRA men Seán Russell and Frank Ryan come to mind since both were alive when Gőrtz began his mission to Ireland on 5 May 1940." He added, for good measure: "a mid-1945 M15 file records that '*in August of that year (1942) he (Frank Ryan) is said to have been received by Hitler*'" McGarry, however, did not engage with such O'Donoghue claims in that 'Hedge School' debate, even though we know that he regards them as nonsensical. Less than three weeks later, on 17 March, *The Irish Times* published his review of Tim Newark's book **The Fighting Irish**, in which McGarry complained of the "finds" cited by that writer. "The chapter on Irish republican involvement with Nazi Germany draws heavily on British military intelligence files without differentiating the occasional factual nugget from the rumours and gossip that comprise most of what is recorded by contemporaneous intelligence sources. Frank Ryan, for example, was not, as described here, a Tipperary journalist, a machine-gun officer, a fervent communist or a Nazi prisoner, and it's highly unlikely that he met Hitler in August 1941." But Newark was only following where O'Donoghue had led. Yet, not alone did McGarry prove unwilling to challenge O'Donoghue himself face-to-face on such nonsense, McGarry reproduced it when placing, without comment, O'Donoghue's March/April 2011 *History Ireland* article – inclusive of that same "Frank meets Adolf" yarn – up on the Queen's University Frank Ryan website as an "Interpretative Source"! To borrow the language of the Romans as they marvelled at the early Christians: See these Irish academic historians – how they love one another! So, it was Newark – the stranger on the shore – who was instead singled out for ridicule.

McGarry, of course, had added insult to injury by trying to associate Kerney's good name with the labelling of Ryan as a *collaborator*. The term *collaborator* – or, alternatively, *collaborationist* – when infused with political meaning, is intended to convey the charge of *treason against one's own country*. It was first deployed with that loaded meaning by the French Resistance, but it only achieved such usage outside France in the post-War era, along with the term *Quisling*, derived from the name of the Nazi puppet ruler of Norway. When Irish military intelligence used the word "collaborate" regarding Ryan in 1941, it had no such treasonous connotation – quite the contrary – and, since there was no direct quote from Kerney, there is no evidence that he himself ever used the word at all, even with its original non-pejorative meaning of "cooperate". In his book, McGarry quoted a G2 (Irish military intelligence) report, dated 20 October 1941, of the debriefing interview with Kerney: "The Minister (Kerney) formed a very favourable opinion of Ryan, he was an idealist and a man of very high principles … The Minister had no doubt that Frank Ryan went willingly to Germany and was apparently anxious to collaborate with the Germans on some basis … He did not believe that Ryan would ever do anything underhand but would be inspired by his desire for the return of the Six Counties as part of the national territory." The only letter Kerney had received by that time that gave any indication of Ryan's hopes and intentions, was a 10 months old one dated 11 December 1940, in which Ryan had expressed the hope that the Germans might cooperate – or collaborate, if you wish – in getting him to the USA. There he would have campaigned among the Irish-American *diaspora* in support of Irish wartime neutrality – to the satisfaction of Germany, no doubt, but from Ireland's point of view, positioning Ryan himself very definitely as the Irish patriot that Minister Kerney declared him to be.

But what of Seán Russell? In a letter in *The Irish Times* on 12 September 2003, I wrote:

> Seán Russell was a man whom de Valera once considered worth making the effort to save from himself. Russell had given sterling service in the 20th century's first war for democracy – the Irish War of Independence, fought to give effect to the democratic mandate of the 1918 elections. When de Valera failed to persuade Russell to accept the democratic mandate of his later Republican election victories of the 1930s, he was left with no option but to act ruthlessly and with resolve against Russell and

Leopold Kerney, Irish Minister to Spain 1935 - 1946
Courtesy: Eamon C. Kerney

his followers. By all means condemn Russell, as I do, for his actions in defiance of de Valera, specifically his 1939 bombing campaign in England, followed by his request for Nazi Germany aid to mount an IRA invasion of the North. If Russell's plan had materialized, it would have led to either a German or British invasion and occupation of Southern Ireland, bringing to naught de Valera's skilful safeguarding of this State from both war and fascism.

But condemnation of Russell is one thing: character assassination is another. Russell was not the Holocaust-champion that Kevin Myers caricatures in his 'Irishman's Diary'. The UK Public Records Office has released files which show that, after intensive post-war interrogation of German intelligence agents at the highest level, British intelligence itself concluded in 1946 that 'Russell throughout his stay in Germany had shown considerable reticence towards the Germans and plainly did not regard himself as a German agent'. In his 1958 novel **Victors and Vanquished**, Francis Stuart observed of the Russell-based character's outspokenness in Berlin: 'Pro-German when it comes to the English, and pro-Jew when it's a question of the Germans'. One might dismiss this as another of Stuart's literary inventions were it not that this assessment was corroborated by a more significant witness – Erwin Lahousen, the first and most important witness for the prosecution at the Nuremberg War Crimes Trials in 1945. Lahousen had been head of the second bureau of the German Intelligence Service (Abwehr) from 1939 to 1943. An Austrian clerico-fascist by conviction, Lahousen loathed Nazism and had been the key figure in an aborted pre-war plot to assassinate Hitler. By common consent, it was Lahousen's evidence at Nuremberg that ensured that Hitler's foreign minister Ribbentrop would be sentenced to death.

It is true that Lahousen's own ideological prejudices led him to make another set of wild and unfounded allegations, such as that Frank Ryan, whom he described as 'a *ruffian of a distinctly red complexion*', had actually murdered Russell. But it is less easy to dismiss what that Nuremberg star witness said of Russell himself. Under the heading of '**No Nazi**', Lahousen's character reference on behalf of Russell was published as follows by *The Irish Times* on 6 June 1958: '*The Irishman was a hyper-sensitive Celt who, however willing he might be to use the Germans for his own political ends, regarded the Nazi philosophy as anathema. To the Austrian Catholic Lahousen, whom he found much more congenial, Russell poured out his private views of the Nazis, their attempts to convert him…Lahousen was sympathetic and took a strong and personal liking to the curious Irishman…He admired his integrity and honesty.*' Lahousen said that '*Russell was the only one of the IRA with whom I dealt who was a real Irish Republican of the old school*'. After what Lahousen described as '*one of Russell's fiery denunciations of the Nazi attempts to indoctrinate him*', the IRA leader further proclaimed: '*I am not a Nazi. I'm not even pro-German. I am an Irishman fighting for the independence of Ireland. The British have been our enemies for hundreds of years. They are the enemies of Germany today. If it suits Germany to give us help to achieve independence I am willing to accept it, but no more, and there must be no strings to the help.*' This was extremely naïve. As regards his dealings with Nazi Germany, Russell is to be condemned more as a fool than a knave. But notwithstanding that condemnation, Seán Russell is still entitled to the integrity of his reputation, in death no less than in life.

Passport Photo of Frank Ryan Taken in Berlin in 1944 a few weeks before his death.
Courtesy: Seán Cronin's "Frank Ryan"

There was, however, a fundamental difference between the respective positions of Russell and Ryan. On 14 May 1942, Frank Ryan in Berlin wrote to Leopold Kerney in Madrid:

England will hang on, fighting to the last Russian and Chinaman, losing all the battles, in the hope of winning the peace…Meanwhile, the attitude of strict (German) respect for (Irish) neutrality continues. Here the policy is one thing at a time; for a year past the West is not mentioned – all attention is concentrated in the opposite direction. The campaign which is now beginning is expected to be decisive. After that? – we'll wait and see.

Ryan had already assured Kerney on 6 November 1941:

My status – that of a non-party neutral – is established…I am not working for – nor even in communication with – any (IRA) organisation at home…There might be a situation in which I might go as a liaison to your boss (Dev)!!! There might also be a situation – I was always a pessimist – in which I might be asked to do something I don't like. Such situation is – soberly speaking – highly improbable. But if the unlikely should ever happen, sit yez down aisy! For – I won't do the dirty. And when you plant my tombstone let it be of granite…Not for nothing did I earn the nickname of 'The Mule' in my school-days!

On 14 January 1942, Ryan further assured Kerney:

In time of national crisis like this, there must be unified command. The country comes before party. So, in his neutrality policy – which is the only sane policy under the circumstances – Dev should get 100% support…Because I know hundreds of good Republicans who are standing aloof today, I am fearful of what may happen if war reaches us. What is the reason for the aloofness of men with fine national records – men like (Ernie) O'Malley; the former IRA chief-of-staff, (Moss) Twomey and the Kerry IRA leader(John Joe) Sheehy…to name but a few? Why aren't they leaders in the (State's) Defence Forces? (Ryan was unaware that Sheehy was actually a Curragh Camp internee at that time)…*As for me – I don't mind the world knowing that here (in Berlin) I do not work for any party or (IRA) organisation, nor am I the successor to any one who has passed away (Seán Russell). I don't mind all this being known, provided at the same time it is known that I'm not either for the Fianna Fáil party.*

Yes, indeed, the essential patriotism of Frank Ryan shines through!

On the issue of Ryan and Germany, there can certainly be an argument for biographical studies that supplement the path-breaking groundwork of Cronin with data from more recently-released official documents from Britain and Ireland. But it is more a case of adding detail to Cronin, rather than differing with him to any great degree as to the substance of relevant material. So, let us again restate the conflicting theses. Was Ryan functioning in Germany as some sort of a Quisling, as O'Donoghue has suggested, a collaborator as McGarry proclaims, part of some secret anti-fascist conspiracy as many on the left still seek to maintain, or a true Irish patriot as others, such as myself, have argued on his behalf? Here again, McGarry's politically compartmentalised chapters allowed for no analysis of Ryan's evolving perspective on foreign policy. McGarry quoted Ryan as saying in August 1931 that in another great war, England's difficulty would once again be Ireland's opportunity, and he argued that there was little reason to think that Ryan's views in this regard changed significantly over the course of the remaining dozen years of his life. But Ryan had, in fact, proceeded from that earlier simplistic viewpoint to develop quite a sophisticated analysis of foreign affairs. McGarry made no mention of the fact that Ryan also used the "England's difficulty" mantra in 1933 on the occasion of Hitler coming to power. **Ah ha!** But, in fact, Ryan's use of that slogan in this instance ran completely counter to the "collaborator" thesis. Ryan had been sufficiently astute to observe that at this juncture Britain was encouraging Germany against France, so that this "Ireland's opportunity" perspective was as much anti-Nazi as it was anti-British. Later still, Ryan appropriated the "We Serve neither King nor Kaiser" slogan in order to counter any Republican temptation to adopt a pro-German position. Finally, yet another detail left completely unmentioned by McGarry was the fact that in 1937, Ryan completely disavowed all simplistic sloganeering when he concluded that the fate of the Wild Geese "should have forever killed the slogan: 'England's enemy is Ireland's friend'."

Ryan's sojourn in Germany must be examined in the circumstances under which it actually unfolded, rather than on the basis of a pre-determined outcome. McGarry's chapter-heading of "Collaborator" required him to adopt a teleological approach that dismissed any evidence that would challenge that verdict. In the only sense in which it remains valid for the term to be used in respect of Ireland, a collaborator can only mean a person who conspired on behalf of Germany against de Valera. No less a witness, however, than the wartime deputy head of Ireland's Department of Foreign Affairs, Frederick Boland, stated quite unequivocally that de Valera himself had indeed sanctioned the release of Ryan in July 1940 from life-threatening prison conditions in Franco's Spain and into the hands of personal friends of Ryan in the German intelligence agency Abwehr, the former left-wing activists Helmut Clissmann and Jupp Hoven. Moreover, British Intelligence files, released in November 2003, contained the January 1946 interrogation of Madrid Abwehr agent Wolfgang Blaum, wherein it was reported: "In May 1940 Blaum was instructed to contact Frank Ryan...who had commanded an Irish volunteer brigade with the Loyalist (Republican) forces in the Spanish Civil War until his capture and imprisonment...Blaum was able to see Ryan in the prison and he persuaded Ryan to go to Germany if he were released. Blaum agreed to Ryan's stipulation that he go to Germany as a free man, and not as a paid German agent. His release was obtained through Admiral Canaris, who saw high Spanish authorities while visiting Spain in Summer 1940. The Spanish officials, however, insisted that Ryan's release be disguised as a prison break."

McGarry dismissed the following argument that is sometimes advanced to suggest that Ryan's purpose in Germany was part of some mysterious anti-fascist conspiracy: "It has been argued that Ryan's presence in Germany was not as anomalous as might seem, since, under the leadership of Admiral Canaris, Abwehr was one of the few pockets of anti-Nazi sentiment. But for most of Ryan's time in Germany, all Irish operations – Abwehr and Foreign Office – were directed by a special department run by Dr. Veesenmayer, an SS Officer on secondment to the Foreign Office." On that point, I quite agree with McGarry's own response, but only insofar as the 1941-44 period is concerned. However, his overall conclusion led him to write quite confusingly about the earlier period of 1940. The significance which he attached to a British intelligence report on the interrogation of Ryan's German handler, Kurt Haller was more preoccupied with formal categorisation than with substance. He quoted not Haller himself, but the language chosen by his interrogator, to sum up for his superiors the following British overview: "By sending Ryan (with Russell to Ireland in August 1940) Abwehr felt that their own interests would be better safeguarded, as Ryan accepted more easily his position as a German agent." McGarry then asked: "Why did Ryan, Ireland's most celebrated anti-fascist, agree to such a course of action?" The British intelligence report, however, was quite clear that Ryan had not been briefed by anybody as to the details of Russell's mission. He had only been hesitatingly accepted by Russell as a fellow-passenger. McGarry made no reference to this hesitation, nor to the fact that two very different sources – the Foreign Office's unrepentant Nazi, Edmund Veesenmayer, who was convicted of war crimes at Nuremberg, and Abwehr's Erwin Lahousen who appeared as a witness for the prosecution at those same Nuremberg trials – both testified that, notwithstanding the warmth of Ryan's and Russell's personal affection for each other, they had, in fact, quarreled politically during their brief German encounter and had been at cross purposes with one another. When Russell died on board the submarine, Ryan returned to Germany rather than land in Ireland. Ryan's own explanation was that he could not bring himself to land in Ireland and tell a suspicious IRA that Russell had mysteriously died in his arms. McGarry, however, wrote of Ryan's decision to return to Germany: "It was this decision which marked a crucial shift in Ryan's attitude...to a conscious determination to collaborate with Nazi Germany...The real question is why, by returning to Germany, did Ryan support republican collaboration with Germany?"

McGarry did not consider that there may well have been a more human, if less heroic, reason for Ryan's decision on the submarine – that the trauma of Russell's death had resulted in a nervous breakdown, accompanied by Ryan's belief that he would only feel safe again in the care of Clissmann who had looked after him when he had crossed the Spanish frontier some weeks previously. For there is parallel evidence from both British and Irish fellow-prisoners that Ryan had previously experienced a similar nervous breakdown shortly after his imprisonment in the Spanish Fascist concentration camp of San Pedro de Cardeña in 1938. Whether his return to Germany initially resulted from such a breakdown or was more politically purposeful from the very outset, we nevertheless have to critically evaluate what it was he was actually doing during the subsequent years spent in that country. McGarry quoted from O'Donoghue's 1989 interview with Francis Stuart concerning the latter's "recall" of a supposed incident in Berlin during 1940: "I never liked Ryan, we didn't really get on…I remember one day…we disagreed over something. He said to me, 'When' – not 'if', mind you – 'Germany wins the war I will be a minister in the Irish Government'. I took this as some sort of threat to me to keep in with him. I took that very much amiss. I didn't like this 'When Germany wins the war'." This, in turn, led O'Donoghue to conclude: "Ryan's comment about becoming a member of the Dublin Government is the clearest indication that what Veesenmayer had in mind was, in fact, a coup d'etat against de Valera." A Quisling, indeed! Unless, of course, we come to the more reasonable conclusion that – in the case of this statement of Stuart's – we are here dealing with a self-serving venomous old viper anxious to foist his own sins on Ryan. For the documentary evidence shows that in 1940 it was not Ryan, but Stuart himself, who was triumphantly proclaiming in his Berlin book on Roger Casement that "the German victory…is, at the moment I am writing these words, almost complete". O'Donoghue's soft interview of Stuart amazingly failed to confront him with the fact that what he was now alleging against Ryan was in direct contradiction with everything else he had written about him over the previous forty years. McGarry left Stuart's slander hanging there. While he questioned Stuart's general credibility, he did not even allude to the earlier Stuart statements that comprehensively refuted that slander. He also failed in the responsibility of a biographer to cross-check with other evidence regarding Ryan's position (and condition) upon his return to Germany in August 1940. In particular, he made no mention whatsoever to a central eye-witness account, that of the unreconstructed Nazi, Róisín Ní Mheara, in her 1992 Irish-language autobiography ***Cé hí seo amuigh?*** She had been Francis Stuart's Berlin mistress during 1940. Due to Helmut Clissmann's absence from Berlin for a period following Ryan's return, Stuart and Ní Mheara were the couple initially charged by the Germans with responsibility for looking after him. Ní Mheara's account remained bitterly antagonistic towards Ryan, as "that hero of Communism who had been sentenced to life imprisonment by Franco as a result of the crimes he had been found guilty of during the Spanish Civil War". She nonetheless recalled just how ill he had been in 1940 and how that illness had been made far worse by the sheer horror of the trauma of experiencing Russell's excruciatingly painful death in his arms under such claustrophobic submarine conditions. Ryan refused to eat. He barely deigned to converse with Stuart. He manifested total distrust of any Germans who came near him and, in fact, used his deafness as an excuse to avoid communication with them. And both Stuart and his Nazi mistress made fun of Ryan's refusal to eat her food, with Stuart sneering: "It's not so much the spy as the fry he is fearing!"

By the end of 1940, Ryan's health had recovered to the extent that he became functional again. If Veesenmayer had any hopes of sending Ryan as a liaison to Ireland in the winter of 1940 before the plans for a German invasion of Britain had been completely shelved, the character of the role that Ryan might have played was quite different from that of Russell. It is strange how McGarry omitted the evidence that showed this clearly to have been the case – the post-war British interrogation of Kurt Haller. For Ryan had indeed decided to become an agent – not, however, on behalf of Germany - but on behalf of Ireland itself. Whereas Russell had asked for German support for an IRA invasion of Northern Ireland (and damn the consequences for de Valera and Southern Ireland), the version of 'Operation Dove' that envisaged a role for Ryan was totally different. McGarry himself wrote that in the event of a German invasion of Britain, the status of Northern Ireland would have been up for grabs. It would have made perfect sense for de Valera to assert his claim to the North with the assistance of German arms rather than accept either a continuing British rule that threatened to invade the South itself, or an extension of German occupation from Britain to Northern Ireland. However, the Haller interrogation revealed that Ryan had completely subverted Russell's own strategy, with the stipulation that there could be no question of any such German assistance being given without the expressed approval of de Valera himself; and that the IRA should in the meantime desist from sabotage operations and confine its activities to agitation and propaganda.

Following Hitler's invasion of the Soviet Union in June 1941 which led to Ryan bluntly telling Veesenmayer that this action had ensured that Germany would lose the War, the threat of a German invasion of either Britain or Ireland receded. Much more threatening was the prospect of an Anglo-American invasion of Southern Ireland. In such an eventuality, the de Valera Government itself (including, expressedly so, Gerald Boland, the very same Minister for Justice who had interned the IRA) made it quite clear that it would accept German assistance to repel such an invasion. And it would be with de Valera himself that Ryan would liaise.

Cronin's pioneering biography had already demonstrated, from the correspondence between Ryan and Leopold Kerney, the Irish Minister to Spain, that Ryan unequivocally pledged his loyalty to de Valera's leadership for the duration of the War. And the Kerney correspondence was the means by which he maintained communication with that leadership. Ryan was Dev's de facto and effective Ambassador in Berlin, vitally needed in that role, not least because of the ineptitude of the official chargé d'affaires, William Warnock. In undertaking that role, Ryan necessarily supped with the Devil, found himself in compromising situations and had to engage in varying degrees of dissimulation. In a 1981 review of Cronin's biography, I had pointed out that the relatively trivial correspondence concerning the wine that Veesenmayer had sent to Ryan as a Christmas gift would have been sufficient to hang him had he lived to experience the post-war Eastern European show trials of former International Brigaders. At times, he found that chalice too heavy to hold. However, as soon as Ryan enquired if he might be discharged from that duty so that he might return to Ireland, de Valera insisted that he stay at his post.

And how did Ryan discharge his duties? Ryan reported to Kerney on how he had protested to Veesenmayer every time there had been a German outrage against Ireland, whether it was the blitz bombing of Belfast, or the more mysterious bombing of Dublin's North Strand, or the sinking of the Irish ship, the "City of Bremen". But Ryan found his protests being skillfully deflected by Veesenmayer who knew how obsequious Warnock had been in undermining the original Irish Government protests. And Ryan also worked particularly effectively in Berlin against the machinations of the very real would-be Irish Quisling, Charles Bewley. Ryan countered Bewley's character-assassination of de Valera and insisted that Dev would remain neutral but fight any invading force, thereby minimizing any temptation in German circles to consider offensive action against Ireland. Furthermore, Kurt Haller's British intelligence interrogator at one point observed of Ryan: "Regarding himself as an Irish patriot and not a creature of the Germans, he refused to associate himself in any way with Hartmann's Irish broadcasts." "Patriot" might well indeed have been the appropriate chapter heading to have used in respect of the final four years of Ryan's life. Patriotism can, of course, also be the last refuge of the scoundrel. But Ryan was no scoundrel. Undoubtedly, he failed to pass the Stalinist test of unconditional loyalty to the interests of the Soviet Union as he also failed to pass the Churchillian test of loyalty to the British Empire. He would have been a prime candidate for a show trial under either regime. But, perhaps an admittedly more insular standard of patriotism will allow us to acknowledge the integrity of the role he played. If he had been a collaborator, de Valera would have been his target. All the more remarkable then that McGarry, while making a passing and dismissive reference to Michael McInerney's 1979 biographical study, *The Enigma of Frank Ryan*, made no mention at all of the one scoop of McInerney's that had eluded Cronin – a 1975 interview with de Valera himself. And in that interview, shortly before his own death, de Valera pronounced: "I am very pleased that you are writing the biography of this great Irishman. Frank Ryan always put Ireland first in everything he did or said, at home or abroad. He has earned his place in history." Ryan had, of course, made clear over the course of his political life that what was good enough for Dev was not good enough for him. But might not what had been good enough for Dev about Ryan himself been also good enough for Ireland? Dev knew how vitally important and essential Ryan's role had been in successfully pursuing his own strategy of safeguarding Ireland from both war and fascism. And yet the German writer Enno Stephan was surely justified in his 1961 pioneering work *Spies in Ireland*, when he observed: "It seems astounding that the Irish Government has up to now done nothing to rehabilitate Franco's one time prisoner, although it could have contributed something to this theme." Only at the end of his own life did the ever-secretive de Valera finally discharge his own duty to do right by Frank Ryan and vindicate his role in Irish history.

Throughout his stay in Germany, as in Ireland and Spain previously, Ryan remained a Connolly Socialist. Indeed, the Spanish Anti-Fascist War never left his thoughts, for in the delirium of his last day on earth, 12 June 1944, Frank Ryan was heard to issue orders in Spanish, as if once more back on the Jarama battlefield. In his own November 1941 pledge to Irish Minister, Kerney – wherein he proclaimed 100 per cent patriotic loyalty and support for de Valera's wartime strategy – Ryan himself had written: "*There might be also a situation…in which I might be asked to do something I don't like…But if the unlikely should ever happen, sit yez down aisy"! For, I won't do the dirty. And when you plant my tombstone let it be of granite – like my stubborn cranium*". And so, fittingly, the tombstone of Frank Ryan in Glasnevin Cemetery is indeed made of granite.

Manus O'Riordan
Ireland Secretary,
International Brigade Memorial Trust

THE SPANISH CIVIL WAR:
AN ANTHOLOGY

'Farewell Spain' by Limerick writer Kate O'Brien
First published by Heinemann in 1937 *by Pamela Cahill*

"As I write Irun is burning…
The café at the corner is a heap of broken stones…
A few men stand around dejectedly with guns"

'*Farewell Spain*' is a clever book written on the eve of the Civil War in Spain (1936-1939) by Limerick-born Kate O'Brien. She takes us to a cluster of cities in Northern Spain and Castile, describing what she likes and highlighting what is at stake should the war continue. It is an easy read for those who know nothing of the war or Spain – yet it is also compelling to readers who have a deep knowledge of both.

The Limerick Writer in Love with Spain

Kate O'Brien (1897-1974) lived in Boru House on Mulgrave Street, Limerick, until the age of five when her mother died from cancer and she became Laurel Hill's youngest boarder. In 1916, the year her father died, she secured a county council scholarship to study English and French at UCD. An avid reader, Kate O'Brien travelled to Spain in 1922 as an English governess and fell in love with the country. She left Bilbao ten months later a changed person and was to spend the rest of her life as a writer based in England – returning to Ireland and Spain when she had the means and the time.

Following a number of literary successes in the UK, in 1936, Kate O'Brien set herself a new and challenging task. Sensing that much in Spain was about to change, she wrote her farewell, which she called "*an occasion of self-indulgence*" to all she knew and loved in Spain. The pro-Republican book was published in London where she lived in 1937. When Franco's Nationalist side won the Civil War in 1939, she had effectively written herself into exile.

Kate O'Brien didn't return to Spain until 1957. During much of that period, she lived in England and wrote novels set in Ireland and Spain as well as working as a literary critic and contributing to both BBC and Radio Eireann radio programmes and newspapers. She returned to the UK when she began to travel back to Spain again more frequently; writing about her trips and her upbringing in Ireland. Kate O'Brien died in Kent in August 1974 aged 76 – one year before Franco's death when Spain's transition to democracy began.

The Skill and Beauty of 'Farewell Spain'

Kate O'Brien was brilliantly placed to write this book – knowing and loving the country as intimately as she did. And being Roman Catholic, although never failing to question and choosing to ignore many of its teachings, provided her with the understanding and the antidote to correctly critique all parties.

Masquerading, as this book can, in the category of sentimental travel memoirs, it should not be underestimated. *Farewell Spain* is actually a carefully-crafted manifesto or plea for sanity in Europe, helpfully and beautifully written in English for an international audience. It's a wake-up call directed at those ignoring the events unfolding in Spain.

Why a Travel Memoir?

The travel guide structure served Kate O'Brien perfectly because it made for a much more approachable read. How much simpler to learn about the conflict on a place by place basis rather than a more political, historical or war-front driven structure? I'm sure she wanted this book to be read very widely. Structured by city or region, she was able to compare and contrast the way of life before and during the Civil War. It was a more personable way to represent events and also a credible way for her to write the book quickly from London. The structure serves both her and her readers very well.

Kate O'Brien by Mary O'Neill (1936)
© Nationall Portrait Galery, London

The People that She Meets

We begin the journey proper in Santander, where I live, and we are treated to many general anecdotes about how to travel and why. We hear about the many happy trips she has made here before bringing us up to date with the political situation.

As we settle in as travelling companions with her, she begins to introduce us to the different sides of the Spanish Civil War. She presents anarchism via Don Angel, the lighthouse-keeper in Santander. She treats him and his ideals with some suspicion and keeps her distance: "*for his lunatic's dream of perfection, he would apply a merciless destruction to all Spain's ages of confused and lovely culture, her indigenous and indescribable faith.* "It must go," Don Angel says, "*it must be martyred, it must be drenched in death.*" But she softens his character by adding, "*As a man may be a fool in Christ, he may be a fool in his brother, and if mad for the love of God, so also mad for the love of man.*"

As we move west, we learn about the writer's religious beliefs. Despite the very recent censorship of her 1936 novel 'Mary Lavelle' in Ireland (it contained scenes of adultery and featured a lesbian character), Kate O'Brien is quite attached to Christian Spain. She criticises the jostling of a priest in Santillana del Mar by two men in overalls and gives the clergyman the upper hand.

I was interested. In the unmistakeably earnest anger of the men, and in the terrier-guts of the little priest. Perhaps he was very cunning… and in the centre of his heart …unafraid of life or death. Anyway it was an interesting round, and went on points to the Church.

In Salamanca, we hear how she despises the burning of the Catholic churches. But she is even more horrified by the anti-clericals who want to save the churches to convert them into markets or garages.

Of course, if there is to be no more praying, if that is done with for ever – the number of empty museum churches, too beautiful to destroy, which Spain will have on her hands, will be a very ludicrous burden. But garages, markets! Oh, Heaven, how humourless people can be, how smugly blind to the strong reality behind life's great expressions! Will they make a dance-hall of Santiago de Compostela?…Give me an anarchist every time rather than these bright, utilitarian dullards.

She is filling in the characters a little more with each new location.

Saints and Communists

When we go to Avila and she writes of Saint Teresa, it might seem that she has been won over by the Nationalist side. But nothing could be further from the truth. She travels back in time to introduce us to a 16th century communist. "*Let no sister have anything of her own but everything in common and to each be given according to her need…all must be equal,*" wrote Teresa. Whether Kate O'Brien was seeking to convince herself or her readers, this was a Kate O'Brien masterly touch. How could we be sceptical or suspicious of a saint?

And so as she travels, she fleshes out Spanish society - from the political to the cultural and the very trivial. We learn what she thinks about Spanish women's hair and make-up, but also her opinions on bullfights and bullfighters.

Along the way, the reader is gradually given reasons to sympathise with the Republican side. We hear early on that the bullfighter, Ortega, was shot. And we worry about Enrique, the young Galician newspaper boy in Santiago de Compostela, who might be now caught up in battle.

The Nationalists in the Shadows

Yet very little is said about Franco and his sympathisers. We are told that Harry in Santander wouldn't be supporting the Republicans but no more is said. The priest in Santillana explains the Republican law removing teaching rights from religious orders but his personal affiliations aren't revealed. And in Asturias, we learn of the Moors.

Franco recruited tens of thousands of Moroccans to fight in the Spanish Civil War. As a fan of Christian Spain, Kate O'Brien tells us she has no time for the Moors, their culture or their architecture. But she didn't confuse her personal sentiments with the facts in Asturias, where she says the Moor never returned "*until Spanish officers marched him up there in October 1934 to shoot at Asturian miners."* She continues to pick away at the Nationalist side and presents us with no coherence or unity, ideological or otherwise.

Madrid's No Pasarán

By the time Kate O'Brien reaches Madrid, we sense the melancholy. We are halfway through the journey and she is by now

reluctant to go forward in search of what is lost. For to talk now of the only Madrid I know – gay, leisurely and moqueur (meaning mocking)– is as if, in the hearing of a friend who has suffered some grievous bodily disaster, one were to discourse of how he was before his day of wounds and mutilations.

It is in Madrid that she makes her case proper for the Republic.

I am not a Communist, but I believe in the Spanish Republic and its constitution, and I believe in that Republic's absolute right to defend itself against military Juntas, the Moors and all interfering doctrinaires and mercenaries. And naturally I believe, as one must, in the Spanish Republic's right to establish itself communistically, if that is the will of the Spanish people. A very large 'if' with which only Spain itself can deal.

Here, Kate O'Brien reminisces about her naivety in Madrid during the summer of 1934. She describes sharing a hotel with Catalan landowners protesting about the Ley de Cultivos - a Catalan Land Commission that never came into being. A transport strike was called to protest against the landowners and the result was the State of Alarm that by October had become a national general strike. Martial law was subsequently declared in Asturias.

To the non-prophetic eyes of a foreigner, this beginning of battle and tragedy did not seem what it was…Indeed, no un-informed looker-on could possibly have guessed that the merrily-conducted protest strike was, and was by the Madrileños understood to be, a significant warning of anger and despair.

Is she forgiving herself for not foreseeing events? Or showing us how innocently it all began? Whatever her motive, I think she had now realised that we, her readers, must be recruited.

She switches from land to culture and writes about the Prado Museum:

The Times shows us photographs nowadays of its stripped and desolate galleries, and we look at them with relief, thankful that the treasures are at present safe from Franco and his allies. That they should have been saved from destruction while children playing nearby in the Calle Atocha had to die is admittedly a bitter gratification, but two wrongs never make a right, and in our tragic day we must take comfort where we can…

Again, Kate O'Brien shows us a heartless Nationalist side.

Kings in Farewell Spain

Just as we are tempted to pigeon-hole the writer into a particular category, she challenges us again. She goes back to the 16th century to reveal her monarchical side. She is in El Escorial (just outside Madrid) and defends Philip II who was "in love with death" and commissioned the palace and its Pantheon of the Kings. She has much less sympathy when observing the empty coffin for Alfonso XIII then in exile *"who now will not be allowed to occupy it"*. Alfonso, in exile, had sided with the Nationalists.

Our final introduction is to the Carlists in Bilbao (a grouping that sided uncomfortably with the Nationalists during the Civil War) which she describes as *"upholders of conservatism, oppression and the divine right of kings"* who have besieged Bilbao unsuccessfully three times, she says, giving it the name Invincible City. She is optimistic about her beloved Basque Country:

Franco's dream of non-representative, non-co-operative government of Spain will not mislead a humorous and reflective Basque. Bilbao may indeed have to face another siege – but she is used to winning them.

The Final Attack

The last chapter is in many ways a summary of the writer's thinking on the different parties involved in the Civil War. Although it is named 'Arriba España', it leaves the reader in no doubt as to which side she supports and her fears for the future if nothing is done.

This twelve page illustration-free chapter is a very painful good-bye letter from Kate O'Brien to Spain – and an angry glare at a world that allows this war to continue.

There is no more to be said. There is nothing left for our sentimental travellers to do but go home and put their suitcases in the attic. And wait for war.

She is clear that democracy must side with the Republicans:

However anti-Communist you may be and however you may deplore the burning of churches or the penalising of the traditional religion of Spain, you cannot, if you take the trouble to read the 1931 Constitution, deny its dignity, justice, humanity, efficiency and natural idealism.

She repeatedly names and attacks Franco:

A war such as General Franco's, openly aimed at the murder of every democratic principle, and for the setting up of his own self as yet another Mussolini – such a war strikes not merely for the death of Spain, but at every decent dream or effort for humanity everywhere.

Yet she wants to leave us with some scrap of hope – telling us that there is still time to respond:

Still, let us be silly and hope while we yet live. Let us dream that the end of everything decent and lovable is not yet. Let us even imagine that Spain, having gone through her hell before our eyes, may actually succeed in giving our nitwitted world the fright and the pause it needs so pointedly, and that, having done us the service of being our cockpit, she may be allowed to heal, crawl back to life and even provide our children's children with some sort of working model of how justice and individualism may flourish together.

The Woman and the Writer

Of course, although a manifesto, it's still a very personal journal, and naturally, some of her opinions are not so easily digested. There's much anti-Moorish sentiment in her musings. And plenty fun poked at the English tourist. And her faith can seem a little out-dated. But while Kate O'Brien can be accused of racism and her own personal faith can be the cause of some head-scratching, she was the most modern of writers. Her own personal life was a balancing act in itself, during which she consistently challenged social boundaries and personally championed the rights of the individual.

She did a great service in writing 'Farewell Spain' and I encourage you to read the book and capture the last breaths of Spain before the worst wounds were inflicted in the Spanish Civil War. Her love for and writings on the country will leave nobody wanting – even 40 years after her own passing.

www.PamelaCahill.com
Santander, Spain

Change is their memorial, who have changed the world. *by Jane Bernal*

Margot Heinemann
1913-1992

At Margot Heinemann's funeral, Tilda Swinton, one of her many remarkable ex-students, read the poem, Ringstead Mill. Margot's final response to the death of John Cornford in Spain in 1936 was written sometime in the last two years of her life - her sister, Dorothy, found it among her papers after she died. In our family tradition, it is words: songs, poems, books; rather than graves that are the true memorials. My mother, Margot Heinemann, has no gravestone but I am proud to be asked to write about her as part of the memorialisation of the brave men of Limerick who fought and died with the International Brigades in Spain.

Margot's connections with Spain and with Limerick were indirect, by way of the men she shared her life with. She used, jokingly, to describe herself as a "Great Man's Moll", referring to her relationships with John Cornford who was killed in Spain in December 1936 and with the great Irish scientist, my father JD Bernal, from 1949 until his death in 1971. Desmond, or Des, as he was known in the later part of his life, came from Nenagh, 23 miles from Limerick and just over the border into Tipperary. Limerick was the nearest large town when he was growing up at the beginning of the last century, and his name is commemorated in Professorial Chairs at the University.

Though Margot is still, perhaps, best known for the dedication of the poem "Heart of the Heartless World" that Cornford sent her from Spain, her life was not defined by the men she knew but by the movement she was part of, and by her own intelligence, humour and resilience. She was intermittently disabled by severe asthma for most of her life but was still writing and supervising students until a few months before her death at the age of 78.

She did not have a planned career but rather a series of interesting jobs that made use of her skills. She worked in further education, for the Labour Research Department (LRD) and then the Communist Party of Great Britain (CPGB). After I was born, she returned to teaching, initially in a school, then a college of education and finally back at Cambridge, the University that awarded her a titular degree in 1934, and to seventeenth century drama, the field of research she had abandoned in 1935 when the Great Depression and the rise of fascism made the study of English Literature feel impossibly irrelevant and self-indulgent.

Family Background

Margot was the middle of three children born to a German Jewish middle-class family in Hampstead in 1913. The family was comfortably off, but, as she put it, "neither rich nor smart". They described themselves as "drawing-room Socialists". In 1926, Margot and her siblings walked to school during the General Strike, their mother explained why they could not use strike-breaking buses. Her immigrant parents placed a high value on education but had less understanding of the British education system. She moved from South Hampstead High School to the open air "progressive" King Alfred School and from there to Roedean, a girl's Public School where she developed a taste for Shelley, Keats and 17th century poetry and an equal distaste for philosophy and the 1920s country house lifestyle of many of her contemporaries. Her sister, Dorothy, stood as Labour candidate in the school mock election in 1929. The sisters ran a terrific campaign and gained 39 votes from a school of 300 odd. Indeed, so successful was their propaganda that when Ramsay McDonald was elected, some girls were afraid that their fathers would be bankrupt and have to sell the hunters!

In 1931, she won a scholarship to Newnham College, Cambridge, to read English. During her first two years, she attended tutorials, played music and acted. She was a member of the cast of *Anthony and Cleopatra* in the first Marlowe Society production to admit women. After the debacle of the 1931 General Election, she attended the odd Socialist society tea but was not politically active. But the rise of fascism in 1933 meant that avoiding serious political engagement no longer seemed an option. In 1934, Margot gained the marks for a First Class degree (though Cambridge at that time did not actually award degrees to women), and was accepted for post-graduate research at Newnham. In the autumn of 1934, she made up her mind to join the Communist Party.

It was no sudden conversion but the result of a year's trying to think her way beyond the traditional pacifism and socialism that she had grown up with to something more effective. (Heinemann, Undated) (Heinemann, 1986).The first political event she was involved with was on Armistice Day 1933 when the peaceful demonstration planned by The Cambridge Student Anti-War Committee was attacked by right-wing militaristic undergraduates and turned into a riot. It made you realise, Margot said, that not everybody was in favour of peace, "Some people are and some aren't. You had to stand up and be counted." The day the Hunger Marchers passed through Cambridge was another turning point for Margot. Wilf Jobling, their leader, was an unemployed miner from Blaydon who was afterwards killed in Spain. His rough but impressive speaking made Margot realise for the first time that "the working- class were not people you led, but were the strength, the power that was going to bring socialism about. They exploited themselves-"Sklaven werden dich befreien"- slaves will set you free, the Brecht song says." (Heinemann, Undated)

It is, I think, significant that Margot joined the Party in 1934 rather than 1933, because of the shift that was taking place within the Communist movement from the very sectarian "class against class" period towards a "people's front". Margot was always a "Popular Front" communist. The party was more attractive to her by late 1934 because it now valued people like her. Her commitment from the beginning was to being part of and serving the working-class movement, in bus strikes, rent strikes or anti-fascist demonstrations. She had no particular interest in either the Soviet Union or in theoretical Marxism, commenting, "I didn't much care for philosophy, even Marxist philosophy." (Heinemann, Undated) Her own Marxism was firmly based in practical reality, historical and economical materialism. She maintained her interest in 17th century poetry,

beginning to see it in a historical context but she had no time for theoretical abstractions and would deflate what she saw as pomposity with alarming accuracy.

John Cornford.

No, not the sort of boy for whom one does
Find easy nicknames, Tommy and Bill,
Not a pleasant bass in a friendly buzz
Of voices we know well,
But not much changing where he goes
Divides talk coldly with the edge of will.

When he began he talked too fast
To be heard well, and he knew too much.
He never had, though learned a little at last,
The sure, sincere and easy touch
On an audience: and his handsome head
Charmed no acquiescence: he convinced and led.

Margot Heinemann
From FOR RJC,
(Summer 1936)

In 1934- 35, the leading communist student in Cambridge was John Cornford, a history undergraduate at Trinity. Margot and John fell in love during the brief intervals between political meetings, her research and his studies for his brilliant First Class degree. In 1935, she left Cambridge for Birmingham to teach at the Day Continuation School at Cadbury's Bourneville. She and John were together for holidays, including one at Ringstead Mill. In the summer of 1936, they were due to meet in the South of France at the beginning of Margot's school holiday when the Spanish Civil War broke out. University terms were shorter. John went to Spain on a press card but rapidly realised that he could not be a bystander in this war and joined the first militia unit he could find. The planned holiday was indefinitely postponed. Margot wrote the poem "For RJC" on the train going back to Paris.

John served first on the Aragon Front. He wrote three remarkable poems there, "Heart of the Heartless World", "A Letter from Aragon" and "Full Moon at Tierz Before the Storming of Huesca". (Cornford, 2006) He brought them back with him when he returned briefly to England in the autumn of 1936 after he fell ill in Spain. He stayed with friends and at Margot's flat in Birmingham while he got together a group of his friends to return with him to Spain. They became the Number 4 section of the Machine Gun Company of the Commune de Paris Battalion and were among the earliest members of the International Brigades. John Cornford was killed at Christmas 1936 in Lopera on or just after his 21st birthday. She was 23.

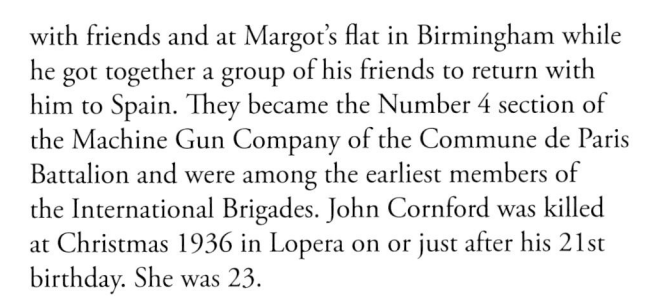

Cornford's short life has been commemorated in many places, for example (Galassi, 1976), (Sloan, 1938) (Stansky & Abrahams, 1994), as well as in three poems by Margot herself, "Grieve in a New Way for New Losses" (1937), "Ringstead Mill" (1991) and the less obviously personal, "This New Offensive" (1938) (Heinemann, 1939). It is tempting, but I believe wrong, to attribute her whole subsequent career, or careers to this personal tragedy. Her communism, her commitment to the working-class movement, had begun before she met John and went on long afterwards.

The Labour Research Department

After John was killed, Margot went down to the Party Centre in London, to confirm that the news was really true. She saw Harry Pollitt, (General Secretary of CPGB) whom she had never met before. He asked if there was anything he could do for her and she asked for a job in the movement, more directly concerned with the fight against fascism or the struggle in the Labour movement. He helped her find a job at the Labour Research Department (LRD) which was, she said, the best thing that could have happened to her. She did not have to pretend to be a worker and yet had the opportunity to use her talents in the service of the working-class movement. She said she learned more from it and enjoyed it more than any work she did later. The friendships she made there remained for life. The research was as rigorous as in any academic department, but the intention was to serve the movement, not to build a CV. The work was largely collective and the researchers left few traces that can be individually attributed.

During the Second World War, she concentrated on the coal industry, working for the LRD alongside men like Arthur Horner, Abe Moffat and Will Paynter, leaders of the Miners Federation of Britain, assembling the detailed evidence that informed both the nationalisation of the coal industry and the formation of the National Union of Mineworkers. From 1949 to 1953, she worked full time for the Communist Party, organising exhibitions, editing books and papers, providing detailed statistics and quotes from the Marxist classics for speakers.

1956 changed everything for her, as it did for all Communists of the period. She remained in the Party but was no longer considered politically reliable. She was no uncritical supporter of the Soviet Union. She also consistently opposed the electoral policy of standing Communists against Labour Party candidates, which she saw as divisive and unrealistic.

John Desmond Bernal

And I thought how I would describe you
To someone who didn't know: and I thought I would say,
This was a man who had the whole universe in his head,
Perfect in little,
As a sailor might have a sailing ship in a bottle
All parts of the model perfect - seas and hills,
Mountains & stars, the green plains & the vast
Unnecessary deserts; and all the works of man,
Houses and scythes, roads riving the ploughlands,
Turbines and towers.
And in the model were also
People, complete down to the last little finger,
Damming the rivers, girding the roaring waters,
And filigree universities & tiny PhD's,
Statues, prayer-wheels & very small bombs,
Missiles & anti-missiles & anti-anti-missile missiles;
The whole thing in motion, endlessly shaping,
Shimmering, fading, transmuting there.
This was a man, I said,
Who had the whole living universe in his head
And did not despair.

Unpublished poem from MCH Archive, undated
Copyright Jane Bernal

Margot and Desmond Bernal met when both were on the Editorial Board of the Modern Quarterly, a Communist periodical, and soon he moved into her flat in Hampstead. In 1953, I was born. Margot was determined to be able to provide for me financially and to find a job that fitted better with the demands of motherhood than full-time political work. She changed her name by deed poll to Bernal and the family moved

Margot and daughter Jane at Mayday parade 1959. JD Bernal just out of picture behind them on left.

to a house in Highgate. When I was tiny, Margot did not go out to work. When I was napping and in one afternoon a week of paid child care she wrote "*The Adventurers*" (published 1959) a novel about a group of intellectuals and young miners at the end of the war and into the 1950s, which fictionalises some of her own experiences and must be one of the few novels ever with a punch-up at the TUC as its dramatic climax.

My father, JD Bernal, 1901-1971 was a lovely man, though I suppose I would say so; a polymath with a lifestory so complicated he said it would have to be written in three colours, black for science, red for politics and purple for his personal life. Again, there are many written memorials (Hodgkin, 1980), (Swann & Aprahamian, 1999), (Brown, 2005). His younger brother, Kevin, inherited the family estate outside Nenagh while Des pursued knowledge in science, history, geology, philosophy and practically everything else. When I was a child, I firmly believed that Da knew everything, though his practical skills at cooking and shopping were pretty limited. At the time when he and Margot became a family, he had been living in London for many years. He was Professor of Physics at Birkbeck and vice-president of the World Peace Council. He travelled all over the world in both capacities, but when he lived in London, he lived with us.

In 1958, Margot began teaching English at Camden School for Girls. Among her pupils, there were the actors Sara Kestelman and Cleo Sylvestre, the authors Julia Donaldson and Deborah Moggach and Vera Gottlieb, later Professor of Drama at Goldsmiths College.

On the Aldermaston March in Easter 1963, Desmond collapsed. Though early tests did not find a cause, by the end of the year he had the first of a series of strokes that were gradually to cripple him, drive him out of scientific and political work and lead to his death in September 1971. As his illness progressed, Desmond's wife, Eileen, returned from the country to help look after him so that he lived with Eileen in Camden Town during the week and with Margot and me in Highgate only at weekends and holidays. In 1965, Margot became a Lecturer in English at Goldsmith's' College, teaching English Literature and supervising students on Teaching Practice. Eric Hobsbawm invited her and her friend Noreen Branson, who still worked at the LRD, to contribute a volume, "Britain in the 1930s" to the Social history series he was editing (Branson & Heinemann, 1971) . They worked together on this in their spare time, in the traditional LRD style, poring over Blue books, company reports and contemporary documents, using secondary sources only when no primary material was available.

Return to Cambridge

Now that she was in higher education, Margot was able to return to 17th Century literature and the subject of the research she had abandoned in 1936, the drama of that other revolutionary period, early Stuart England. In 1975, she published a monograph for English Literary Renaissance on "*Puritanism and Theatre*" (Heinemann, 1980). Real politics, then as now, were more complicated than that. Many plays were dedicated to Puritan patrons; some actors and playwrights had Puritan sympathies; and Puritan pamphleteers were full of theatrical ideas. As a result of this ground-breaking work, she was invited back to Cambridge where she ended her official career as a College Lecturer at New Hall.

The renaissance of left-wing politics among students in the 1960s and 70s delighted her. Though she saw some of what was going on as an oversimplification and was as critical as ever of theoretical "bull-shit", she was excited by the energy of it and always loved being with young people. She participated in demonstrations against the Vietnam War and the Apartheid regime in South Africa, enjoyed the revitalisation of Marxism Today and was one of the earliest supporters of the Communist University of London. Suddenly, her type of politics was in favour again, she became a member of the Party's Theory and Ideology Committee, commenting, "The stone that the builders rejected is become the keystone of the whole arch."

She was somewhat bemused by the recurrence of interest in the 1930s and in herself as a living relic of that period. However, it gave her and her fellow survivors the opportunity to try to set the record straight with a new generation. As she and her co-editors wrote in the foreword to "*Culture and Crisis in Britain in the Thirties*", it seemed important "to correct some of the commoner misunderstandings and distortions" and to show that thirties' culture was not "just a small group of poets talking to one another, or that the whole radical and revolutionary impetus faded out in 1939, leaving not a rack behind." (Clark, et al., 1979) She was in demand for lectures on Shakespearean Tragedy, Censorship and Patronage in 17th Century theatre and on the poetry of the Spanish Civil War. When she read and analysed "Full Moon at Tierz" there was, as she said, not a dry eye in the house.

After her official retirement in 1981, she continued to teach both at Cambridge and more widely as much as her failing health would allow. She had intermittent breathing problems all her life and these became much worse after contesting the 1951 general election for Lambeth in the London smog of that year. From that time onwards, chronic bronchitis and acute asthma took her into hospital most winters, though she was able to climb mountains in the clear air of the West Highlands in the summer. My parents first visited the Coigach peninsula in Wester Ross in the early 1960s and Margot returned there many times. In her seventies, Margot delighted in showing the beaches, waterfalls and the distinctive sky-line of Stac Pollaidh to her beloved grandson, Sam. By 1992, the cumulative effects of the years of her illness and the steroids prescribed to combat it were too much for her. She died in London on June 6th 1992. Her ashes are scattered on the summit of Stac Pollaidh.

Her last essay, published in that year, was, "God Help the Poor, The Rich Can Shift": The World Turned Upside Down and the Popular Tradition in the Theatre. (McMullan, 1992)

'*The challenge*,' she said in 1991, to those of us who still want to change the world, '*is to take up the shamed, blood-stained cause of the Left and make it what it was meant to be, and not what 65 years of misuse and error have made it. That's where I stand.*'

BIBLIOGRAPHY

Branson, N. & Heinemann, M., 1971. *Britain in the 1930s.* London: Weidenfeld & Nicolson.

Brown, A., 2005. *J.D. Bernal: The Sage of Science.* 1 ed. Oxford: Oxford University Press.

Clark, J., Heinemann, M., Margolies, D. & Carole, 1979. Forward. In: *Culture and Crisis in Britain in the 1930s.* London: Lawrence & Wishart, pp. 7-11.

Cornford, J., 2003. *Full Moon at Tierz*: Before the Storming of Huesca. 1 ed. Nottingham: Five Leaves Publications.

Cornford, J., 2003. *Poem.* Nottingham: Five Leaves Publications.

Cornford, J., 2006. *A Letter from Aragon.* 1 ed. London: Lawrence & Wishart.

Cornford, J., 2006. *Three poems.* 1 ed. London: Lawrence & Wishart.

Galassi, J., ed., 1976. *Understand the Weapon Understand the Wound*: selected writings of John Cornford. 1 ed. Manchester: Carcanet.

Heinemann, M., 1939. *Grieve in a New Way for New Losses.* London: The Hogarth Press.

Heinemann, M., 1939. *This New Offensive.* London: The Hogarth Press.

Heinemann, M., 1980. *Puritanism and Theatre.* 1 ed. Cambridge: Cambridge University Press.

Heinemann, M., 1986. *IWM 9239/5* [Interview] 1986.

Heinemann, M., Undated. *Margot Kettle Interviews* [Interview] Undated.

Hodgkin, D., 1980. *John Desmond Bernal. Biographical Memoirs of Fellows of the Royal Society*, December, Volume 26.

McMullan, G., ed., 1992. "God Help the Poor, The Rich Can Shift": The World Turned Upside Down and the Popular Tradition in the Theatre. In: *The Politics of Tragi-comedy, Shakespeare and After.* London: Routledge.

Sloan, P., 1938. *John Cornford A Memoir.* 1 ed. London: Jonathan Cape.

Stansky, P. & Abrahams, W., 1994. *Journey to the Frontier: Two Roads to the Spanish Civil war.* Constable ed. London: s.n.

Stansky, P. & Abrahams, W., 2012. Julian Bell: *From Bloomsbury to the Spanish Civil War.* 1 ed. Stanford: Stanford University Press.

Swann, B. & Aprahamian, F. eds., 1999. *J.D.Bernal: a Life in Science and Politics.* 1 ed. London: Verso

Heart of the Heartless World
and
Ringstead Mill

John Cornford and Margot Heinemann

John Cornford, born in 1915, was one of the early British volunteers to go to Spain. He had a privileged background and was the great grandson of Charles Darwin. Shortly after graduating from Cambridge with 1st class honours, he left for Spain in August 1936 to fight for the Republican cause. He fought in the battles for Madrid and Boadilla and was killed in December 1936 on the Córdoba Front on or just after his 21st birthday. Shortly before his death, he wrote his much acclaimed "Poem" which was addressed to Margot Heinemann. It is a tender love letter that is all the more poignant given his subsequent fate. It remains one of the most memorable and widely-read love poems of the 20th century.

About a year before she died in 1992, Margot Heinemann penned a beautiful response to John Cornford's "Poem" in her evocative "Ringstead Mill". They had spent happy times at Ringstead Mill, a six-story windmill, Cornford's home in Norfolk.

John Cornford

Poem

Heart of the heartless world,
Dear heart, the thought of you
Is the pain at my side,
The shadow that chills my view.
The wind rises in the evening,
Reminds that autumn is near.
I am afraid to lose you,
I am afraid of my fear.
On the last mile to Huesca,
The last fence for our pride,
Think so kindly, dear, that I
Sense you at my side.
And if bad luck should lay my strength
Into the shallow grave,
Remember all the good you can;
Don't forget my love.

John Cornford
1936

Ringstead Mill

Stranger whom I once knew well,
Do not haunt this house.
Sorrow's but a ravelled thread,
To draw back the active dead,
Nor is pleasure mutable
Such as smiled on us.
Stranger whom I once knew well,
Do not haunt this house.

Idle and low spirits can
Take your name and face:
Old green sweater, battered coat,
Coal-black hair and sleeves too short.
Though I know the living man
Finished with this place,
Idle and low spirits can
Take your name and face.

Here we laid foundations where
Never walls were built.
Faded is the fireside glow,
Things we knew or seemed to know
Blown around the empty air,
And the milk is spilt.
Here we laid foundations where
Never walls were built.

And the hard thing to believe
Still is what you said.
With a bullet in the brain,
How can matter think again?
All things that once live and move
Endlessly are dead.
And the hard thing to believe
Still is what you said.

So from these deserted rooms,
Even memory's past.
As your closely pencilled screed
Grows more faint and hard to read,
So our blueprints and our dreams,
Torn from time are lost.
So from these deserted rooms,
Even memory's passed.

Mountains that we saw far off,
Sleek with gentle snow,
To the climbers axe reveal
Ice that jars the swinging steel,
Armoured on a holdless cliff
With the clouds below -
Mountains that we saw far off,
Sleek with gentle snow.

Time bears down its heroes all
And the fronts they held.
Yet their charge of change survives
In the changed fight of our lives -
Poisoned fires they never dreamed of
Ring the unrented field.
Change is their memorial
Who have changed the world.

Margot Heinemann
1991

From Limerick to Brunete: the Curious Story of George Nathan

by Melody Buckley

Why write about George Nathan? Seventy-seven years after his death, he is celebrated as the brave and enigmatic Englishman who fought in the Spanish Civil War and died in the Battle of Brunete on the 26 of July 1937. He has been described as "the only personality serving in the International Brigades who emerges as an authentic hero figure, with a mythology of his own". A number of individuals of all nations behaved magnificently but none of them had the essential larger than life quality that distinguished George Nathan."[1] There is also the exciting story of his true adventures in the British Army from 1913, when he joined the army at 16 years of age to escape a dreary fate as a butcher in London's East End, to his capture and imprisonment by the Germans during the Battle of Arras,[2] one of the bloodiest battles of the War. But, as well as this bright, heroic aspect, George Nathan had a darker side. As part of the British Intelligence apparatus, he engaged in clandestine activities such as the high-profile murders of the mayors of Limerick (the Curfew Murders)[3] during the Irish War of Independence in 1920-1921.

Historical events combined with an unusual and dysfunctional family history shaped George Nathan's complex personality. He was born on 21 December 1896 to unmarried parents, Samuel Levy Nathan, aged 43 and Jane Annie Maud Frost, aged 23, in Hackney, London.[4] His father was Jewish, while his mother was half Protestant, half Catholic. Her Irish mother, Annie Lacy, was born in Cork during the famine.[5] They baptised their son at the Church of St Mark in Victoria Park,[6] raising him as Church of England, although throughout his life, he would identify as either Jewish or Church of England, depending upon the circumstances. George Nathan was part of a generation of men born in the late 1890's who became battle-hardened; they lost their youth and idealism in the war, while living through the societal changes wrought by it. The army gave some of these young men the rare chance to experience upper-class life. When officers were desperately needed, brave men like George Nathan were temporarily commissioned from the

George Nathan
Photo courtesy: www.pdlhistoria.wordpress.com

ranks and were given the same privileges and deference as the upper-class officers. When the war ended and these "temporary gentlemen"[7] had outlived their usefulness, they were unceremoniously decommissioned. However, Nathan, having developed a cultivated accent (he was an excellent mimic) and a taste for the upper-class lifestyle, was more fortunate. After the war, he was sent to an isolated Indian outpost,[8] where he remained for less than one year before voluntarily accepting a most lucrative opportunity which he expected would not only help him contribute more to support his family, but would also keep him in the style to which he had become accustomed.

On the 20 October, 1920, George Nathan arrived in Ireland during the height of the Irish War of Independence. He had been hired to work in British Intelligence as an Auxiliary Cadet attached to the Irish police force (the Royal Irish Constabulary).[9] He was one of many Auxiliaries who had been "temporary gentlemen." Most of these, including Nathan, were not politically motivated.[10] If they found it difficult to carry out orders, e.g., raids, house searches, property damage, and sometimes assassinations and collateral murders, they rationalised that they were following orders, and tried to stifle any pangs of conscience with thoughts of the financial incentives, and often, an excessive amount of alcohol. While they fully expected to be part of a militarised police force, they were ill-prepared for the work they were required to do. Upon leaving Ireland on the 30 April, 1921 without his commission, Nathan re-enlisted in the army twice, as a private, first with the West Yorkshire Regiment in 1921, then with the Royal Fusiliers, in 1925.[11]

Throughout his life, George Nathan was always on the outside, looking in. He stood outside the realm of normalcy for the times, not only for reasons of his individualistic personality, but also by virtue of his religious background and sexual orientation. But while his interfaith background caused him some difficulty, it paled in significance to the problems arising from his sexual orientation. While in Ireland, for example, a contemporary described him as "a typical Jewboy" and a "raging homosexual."[12] In an interesting twist of the truth, the portion of the statement describing him as "a typical Jewboy" was false, while the homosexual comment, although negatively cast, was true. His army career ended abruptly in 1926, when he was discharged from the army with ignominy[13] for a crime related to his homosexuality. After the loss of his army career, he was on a downward spiral of alcoholism and hopelessness, wandering through dead-end jobs, traversing Canada and the United States,[14] sometimes as a hobo, until he volunteered for battle in the Spanish Civil War in November, 1936, one month short of his 40th birthday[15] and probably as a chronic alcoholic. With no stable future employment possibilities, Nathan held onto the dream that in this battle, he would somehow find his place in the world, back in an army and fighting against fascism.

Although his heroic aspect shone brightly in Spain, George Nathan shrouded his past in his most precious possession, a special mystique he created for himself. From the time he arrived in Spain until his death seven months later, as he rose up through the Brigades hierarchy, George Nathan recounted his own version of the story of his past, for all who would listen. He was a poor, East End Jewish lad of little education, who by dint of hard work was commissioned as the only Jew in the Brigade of Guards during WW1. There, he developed his cultivated accent and manners but fell upon hard times as a result of his socialism - his refusal to allow the men under his command to be treated unfairly.[16] The more cynical and worldly men thought this story too good to be true. Some of them, who had actual knowledge of his past, knew it to be absolutely false. The posh accent never sounded quite right. In reality, bits of truth were woven within layers of fantasy and wishful thinking. George Nathan enjoyed using his imagination, exaggerating and embellishing the truth, which was sometimes purely for effect, but at other times, to conceal or obfuscate the truth. For example, his tale of membership in the Brigade of Guards was a many-levelled ruse: it obscured his true WW1 experience, his heroism as well as his subsequent discharge with ignominy, and it also may have alerted men to his sexual preference.[17] However, neither his heroic nature nor this special mystique were evident upon his arrival at International Brigade Headquarters in Albacete, in south eastern Spain with the Jewish War Veterans' Group in December, 1936. To the other mostly British volunteers, he appeared an unshaven hobo; the only glimpse into a different past was his immaculately-pressed army uniform which he carried with him. But cleaned up in his uniform in the new boots given to him by the Irish volunteer, Frank Ryan, glittering in the sun, with his obvious military bearing and cultivated accent, he quickly metamorphosed into the elegant, fastidious gentleman everyone would remember.[18]

At the basic training camp in Madrigueras, near Albacete, George Nathan was elected Captain of the No.1 Company of the XIVth Brigade over the objection of some of the Irish volunteers who remembered him from the War of Independence. An English volunteer, Walter Greenhalgh, said that the matter of George Nathan's past was discussed when a number of Irish men announced to the group that they did not want this "Black and Tan" to be in charge.[19] The election of George Nathan as Captain of the No. 1 Company, which included British and Irish volunteers, was clearly a controversial choice in light of his earlier history. But his selection not only supported the socialist ideology that individuals renounce national loyalties to unite in the battle against fascism but also made sense given his extensive military experience. And not all of the Irish Volunteers refused to serve under him. Frank Ryan, the subject of several biographies and ongoing scholarly research,[20] supported George Nathan's leadership. Ryan, who was from Co Limerick and a teenager in 1921, would have been aware of George Nathan's connection with British Intelligence. In a 1996 handwritten letter to the Limerick historian, Des Ryan, the Waterford volunteer Peter O'Connor wrote: "Nathan was one of the greatest soldiers who took part in the fight against fascism in Spain." He added: "Frank Ryan thought very highly of him [George Nathan] and regarded him as a friend, comrade and fellow officer in the fight against fascism. What Frank Ryan thought of Nathan was good enough for all of the members of the Connolly Column."[21] However, while it is only third-hand evidence, it is quite a believable story that in January, 1937, after the Battle of Lopera, the Irish volunteers convened an informal court intending to sentence him to death. At this inquisition, he allegedly admitted to being in the service of the Crown and carrying out the Crown's orders. His life was saved, possibly by his own explanations, possibly by the timely intervention of their leader, Frank Ryan.[22]

On the 26 of July, 1937, George Nathan was fatally wounded by a splinter bomb at the conclusion of the Battle of Brunete. Steve Nelson, an American Commissar commandeered an ambulance at gunpoint to take the wounded man to the hospital where he died of his injuries.[23] They buried him in state in darkness, and even his enemies wept. At the funeral, George Aitken, Commissar of the XVth International Brigade recited the heroic poem, "The Burial of Sir John Moore after Corunna."[24] But his heroic send-off was subsequently tarnished. Twenty-four years after George Nathan's death, an article appeared in the New Statesman Magazine, in which, two men who had been with the Auxiliaries in Ireland implicated George Nathan in the murder of the Mayors of Limerick in 1921. The author ended the article with the question: "What was the ex-member of the Dublin Murder Gang doing in the International Brigade? Expiating his past? Or, like many another, just playing a part to death?"[25] These questions inspire the beginning of a search to understand the complex psychology of this unique man.

Endnotes

1: Gurney, Jason. *Crusade in Spain*. London: Faber and Faber, 1974, p. 93.

2: Kew, Surrey, UK, The National Archives of the UK (TNA), Public Record Office (PRO): *Army Service Records*, War Office, First World War, Personal Files. Lieut. GSM Nathan, WO 374/50047. George Nathan enlisted in the Duke of Cornwall's Light Infantry as a trainee in the Special Reserves on 9 January 1913. Email correspondence from Major Trevor Stipling, Curator, Duke of Cornwall Light Infantry Museum, Bodmin, Cornwall, dated 17 May 2006. 2nd lieutenant GSM Nathan of the 2nd Battalion of the Royal Warwickshire Regiment was listed as missing in action on 5/3/17. Copy of Battalion diary kindly provided by Mr. David Baynham, Attendant at the Royal Regiment of Fusiliers Museum, St. John's House, Warwick, UK, on 3 April 2006.

3: Website on the Limerick City Curfew Murders: http://www.limerickcity.ie/media/Curf001.pdf. They were called the Curfew murders because they took place after 10PM when the population of Limerick were prohibited from leaving their homes.

4: Southport, UK, General Register Office, *Certified copy of an Entry of Birth*, District of Hackney, Vol. 1b, p. 623. George Nathan's parents subsequently married on the 8th of August, 1899.

5: TNA PRO, *Census Returns of England and Wales*, 1871, RG10/123, Folio 5, pg. 1.

6: London Metropolitan Archives, *Register of Baptisms* St. Mark, Victoria Park, , Oct. 1893-May 1898, p. 188/mrk015.

7: Wheatley, Dennis, *The Time has Come: The Memoirs of Dennis Wheatley: 1914-1919: Officer and Temporary Gentleman*, London: Hutchinson and Company Ltd, 1975; James, Lawrence. *Warrior Race: A History of the British at War*. London: Abacus, 2001, pp. 552-553.

8: TNA PRO: *Army Service Records*, WO 374/50047.

9: TNA PRO: *Home Office Records of the Royal Irish Constabulary* for temporary constables who served with the auxiliaries, HO/184/51/325. I am grateful to Richard Abbott, author of Police Casualties in Ireland, 1919-1922, Mercier Press, 2000, for further explaining these records.

10: Glesson, James. *Bloody Sunday*. London: Peter Davies Ltd. 1962. p. 62.

11: TNA PRO: *Army Service Records*, WO 374/50047.

12: Bennett, Richard, Portrait of a Killer, *The New Statesman*, 24 March 1961, 1, pp. 471-472.

13: TNA PRO Army Service Records, WO 374/5004.

14: Ancestry.com. *Border Crossings: From Canada to U.S., 1895-1956* [database on-line]. Provo, UT, USA: Ancestry.com Operations, Inc., 2010. Original data: *Records of the Immigration and Naturalization Service, RG 85*. Washington, D.C. Other information from Ancestry.com: Canadian Passenger Lists, 1865-1935, UK outward (1890-1960) and incoming (1878-1960) passenger lists.

15: TNA PRO, Security Service Files, *British Volunteers*, KV5/112

16: Many volunteers believed this story, e.g. Walter Greenhalgh, Imperial War Museum (IWM), London, Sound Archive, 11187/2. See also, Thomas, Hugh, *The Spanish Civil War*, New York: Random House, revised edition 1989, p.476. Earlier editions (1961) provided more detail about George Nathan's Brigade of Guards story.

17: Houlbrook, Matt, Soldier heroes and rent boys: Homosex, masculinities and brutishness in the brigade of guards, circa 1900-1960. *Journal of British Studies*, July 2003, 42/3, pp. 351-368.

18: Monks, Joe, *With the Reds in Andalusia*, London: John Cornford Poetry Group, 1985

19: IWM, London, Sound Archive, Walter Greenhalgh, 11187/9.

20: Hoar, Adrian, *In Red and Green, the lives of Frank Ryan*, Dingle, Bandon Books, 2004; McGarry, Fearghal, *Irish Politics and the Spanish Civil War*, Cork, Cork University Press, 1999; and Stradling, Robert, *The Irish and the Spanish Civil War*, Manchester: Manchester University Press 1999.

21: Wharton, Barrie, ed. The Spanish Civil War Archive, Limerick: University of Limerick, 2002

22: Levine, Maurice. *Cheetham to Cordova: A Manchester Man of the Thirties*. Manchester: N. Richardson, 1984, p. 39.

23: Nelson, Steve. *The Volunteers, A Personal Narrative of the Fight against Fascism in Spain*, Masses and Mainstream, 1953, pp 166-170.

24: IWM, London, Sound Archive, George Aitken, 10357/2, Wolfe, Charles. "*The Burial of Sir John Moore at Corunna.*" 1817.

25: Bennett, Richard, Portrait of a Killer, *The New Statesman*, 24 March 1961, p. 472.

Ned Vallely aka Peter Brady

by Ger McCloskey

As this book is entitled *From the Shannon to the Ebro*, it would be remiss of us not to mention a man, although not born in Limerick- he spent most of his adult life here - Edward "Ned "Vallely, born in Cavan near the source of the Shannon River – an International Brigadista.

Ned was born on the 23 May 1914 and emigrated to London in the early 1930s where he became politicised. Whilst information on his time in Spain is sparse, we have gathered the following information:

He joined the International Brigades on 25 December 1937 under the pseudonym Peter Brady (his mother's maiden name) and was with the 3rd Recruits Company in the British base in Tarragona.

Bob Doyle recounts in his book *Brigadista* being strafed by Italian fiat fighter planes in the olive groves outside Belchite during the Aragon retreats in March 1938 with Peter Brady and Johnny Lemon. After withdrawing from that town towards Calaceite, they were joined by Frank Ryan who had come up from Madrid having finished writing his book *The History of the Fifteenth International Brigade*. The group which also included Limerick man Gerard Doyle was ambushed and surrounded by Italian fascist soldiers from the Black Arrow division. Over 100 men were taken prisoner and many more killed. These prisoners were taken firstly to Saragossa for interrogation and then transferred to the notorious prisoner-of war-camp of San Pedro de Cardeña. Conditions in the camp eleven miles south of Burgos were horrific. Peter (Ned) was held here until early 1939 when he was released with the majority of British and Irish prisoners in exchange for Italians held by the Spanish Republic.

Ned moved to Sixmilebridge in 1940 to work on the new Shannon Airport. He married Eta Houlihan from Loughrea Co. Galway, and moved to Limerick in 1957 where they had five children: Joe, Eddie, Michael, Jim and Eta junior. Having worked for Murphy Bros. Builders for over thirty years, Ned passed away on the 30th of January 1975 in his adopted town.

Thanks to the Working-Class Movement Library for use of the picture of Peter.

Following release from prison, being fitted out in London for new clothes by the Dependent's Aid Committee: Peter Brady with an address shown as Co. Cavan on extreme left back.

Reginald Watkins

by Bill Watkins

My father, Reginald Watkins, was born in Wales in 1920 and was a Welsh-speaker. He left school at 15 and became an engine-cleaner and later a fireman on the Great Western Railway in Wolverhampton where he joined ASLEF, The Associated Society of Locomotive Engineers and Firemen. His intention was to go to night-school and eventually enrol in Art College to study fine art and drawing, but after attending a Union event centred on the war in Spain, his plans changed. Reg became interested in Celtic culture and republican politics. Dismayed at the official Labour Party's pro-UK leanings, he was drawn to the more Independent Labour Party, as were many Scots, Irish and Welsh Nationalists.

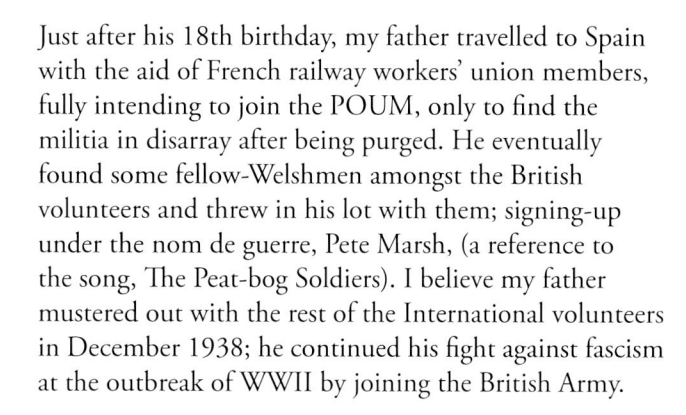

Reg with his family.

Just after his 18th birthday, my father travelled to Spain with the aid of French railway workers' union members, fully intending to join the POUM, only to find the militia in disarray after being purged. He eventually found some fellow-Welshmen amongst the British volunteers and threw in his lot with them; signing-up under the nom de guerre, Pete Marsh, (a reference to the song, The Peat-bog Soldiers). I believe my father mustered out with the rest of the International volunteers in December 1938; he continued his fight against fascism at the outbreak of WWII by joining the British Army.

During the war, he met my mother, Monica McDonagh from Thomodgate, Limerick, she was working in Birmingham at the BSA factory making Bren guns. They married in 1949 and settled near Stratford-upon-Avon. Occasionally, when I was a child, some of his old comrades from the Spanish era would come to visit; Jack Rouse, a London house-painter was one, a big Irishman called MacBride was another. They would talk about Teruel and Ebro and Alicante and other places I'd never heard of. Reginald retired in the early 1980s and spent much of his later years in Limerick as a regular at the Ardnacrusha Bar in Thomondgate, he kept in contact with a few of his Irish pals from the old days. Anytime I popped into Connolly Books in Dublin, Mícheál O'Riordan would ask after him. Reg died in 1986, his ashes were scattered on the river Lugg, Bleddfa, Wales, the Shannon at Killaloe and the Ebro near Zaragoza.

Irish Women's Admirable Involvement in the Spanish Civil War

by Muireann Hickey

Winning Essay in the Friends of the International Brigade Spanish Civil War Essay 2013 for Secondary School Students in Ireland

At the beginning of the Spanish Civil War, the Irish Government ignored the fact that hundreds of Irish people were volunteering to fight both for and against the fascists of General Franco. According to a government memo published the previous December in the *Irish Examiner*, De Valera's government was warned "not to make martyrs out of the Irish men and women who fought and died in the Spanish Civil War".[1] This war is now seen by many historians as the prelude to World War Two and the fight against fascism.

It is thought that around one thousand people from Ireland fought in the Spanish Civil War in an astonishing show of international solidarity to defend democracy. Figures suggest that seven hundred and fifty people joined the Blueshirts and two hundred and seventy seven people fought with the International Brigades.[2] Many people mistakenly believe that everyone who joined Eoin O'Duffy was a fascist. Some may have been, but the vast majority of those who did fight for Franco had no interest in fascism and were more traditional Catholics. However, many of the people who joined O'Duffy, especially from Belfast, did so because of the fact that they were devout Catholics and, as a consequence, did what the Church told them to do, but they also went to fight because of the unique relationship they had with O'Duffy himself.[3]

While details of the Irish men who fought in the Spanish Civil War are well documented, Irish women's role in the war is rarely highlighted. However, we do know that women worked hard as nurses and solidarity workers collecting food and funds for Spain both in Ireland and in Spain.

The Women's Aid committee was set up by Hanna Sheehy-Skeffington (Born in Kanturk, Co. Cork), who was renowned for her work in the Irish suffrage movement and who was the committee's chairperson. The aim of this committee was to create and maintain a fund for Basque war victims. The National Library of Ireland has a copy of a letter signed by Sheehy-Skeffington and issued by the Women's Aid Committee, soliciting contributions from "Irish friends of the Spanish Republic" in order to maintain a fund for Basque war victims.[4]

Other prominent members of the Women's Aid Committee included writer and historian, Dorothy MacArdle (Born in Dundalk, Co. Louth) and Nora Connolly-O'Brien (Born in Scotland but shortly after moved to Ireland), daughter of James Connolly.

According to the historian, Rob Russell, trained nurses were in very short supply in Spain because before the war this work was chiefly done by nuns, and so there was often a heavy reliance on foreign medical volunteers. This reliance highlights the important role that women played in the Spanish Civil War.

Angela Jackson wrote a book that documents and gives analysis to the role that British women played in the war. Some of the women that Angela wrote about had Irish links, for example, Rose Kerrigan who was born in Ireland. Rose married Peter Kerrigan who joined the International Brigades. She was active in solidarity work collecting for Spanish relief and she fully supported her husband when he became a political commissar to the International Brigades.[5]

Another interesting woman who was in some way involved in the civil war was Ruth Ormesby who was born in Dromore, Sligo. In the second week of August 1937, a mobile hospital was set up at La Puebla de Hijar, near Quinto. One calculation based on IBA records estimates that she arrived in Spain on April 16th 1937. The "English nurses… and Ruth Ormesby turned four wooden huts which had no electricity or water supply into a hospital." Ormesby was a Roman Catholic, who was killed while staying in the Medical Aid flat in Barcelona. She and a Spanish nurse were making tea when the primus stove exploded and the room caught fire. They tried to escape and fell from a window, Ruth to her death. It is said that she died in April 1938, but delays in receiving the news meant that the local papers in Northern Ireland, *The Irish News, News Letter* and *Belfast Telegraph* only carried a report from London on 11th of May 1938, saying that Hannah Ruttledge Ormesby had died in an accident while serving with the

British Medical unit in Spain.[6] It is also believed that she was the only Irish woman who died out in Spain.

While carrying out my research, another woman's name that seemed to pop up was that of Katherine Lynch. A letter to Tom O'Brien in Spain, dated 2nd August 1938 said " Doctor Lynch is now in Perpignan doing some hospital work and she may be useful in getting the (cigarettes) across". Although Perpignan is in France, she was obviously providing aid for the republican cause and so is included. Katherine Lynch was a very hard worker and seemed passionate about what she did. Peadar O'Donnell says that she "did such Trojan work for the Republican cause in critical days when the winning of influential American opinion was so vital."[6]

Another prominent figure with regard to Irish women's involvement in the Spanish Civil War was Beatrice de Courcy. She was born to parents of Irish descent and was married to Dr. John de Courcy (historian and political activist). She had paramedical training with the Red Cross and St. John's Ambulance. According to her obituary which appeared in the Irish Times on January 8th 2000, de Courcy volunteered to go to Barcelona with a medical team in support of the International Brigades. She also spoke at many rallies on her way home.[7] Her husband wrote to Ciarán Crossey saying that his wife had travelled to Spain in a delegation from Manchester:

> with a large quantity of medical supplies of which my wife was in charge. My wife had learnt a lot of Catalan and a lot about the Catalan political movement and was evidently a great favourite in Barcelona where she spoke several times on the Republican radio to all of Spain emphasising her sympathy as an Irishwoman with the national movements, Catalan, Basque, etc. in Spain (Barcelona was bombed while she was there) Manchester, Bolton, Liverpool and a particularly huge one in Bradford[8]

Charles Patrick "Charlie" Donnelly was an Irish poet and left- wing political activist. He was killed fighting on the republican side during the Spanish Civil War. However, a woman who is forever linked with him is Cora Hughes. She came from a well-respected republican family – her godfather was Eamon de Valera. She also had studied in UCD and became commander of the Cumann na mBan division on campus. Although she did not go to Spain, she was a tireless worker in support of the Spanish Republic. She was jailed in September 1934 for her work in supporting rent strikes in Dublin. She was described as a "tireless housing activist" but unfortunately she died tragically in 1940 after contacting TB in the slums.[9]

When we visualise war, we imagine brave, prestigious, patriotic men going out to fight. You could say those perceptions are true, however, we sometimes tend to forget what hard work goes on outside the battlefield, or what aid is given to the injured or what cunning plans are being thought up by those in the background. We really do tend to forget about the importance of women in times of war and emergency. The actions of women in the war era posed a significant challenge to their traditional roles as guardians of the home. For example, the very prominent *Mujeres Antifascists*, a coalition of women from a variety of leftist political groups, was formed with the mission of removing the Spanish woman from the state of ignorance to which patriarchal society had relegated her.

Many iconic and empowering women have succeeded in many walks of life and are lauded and remembered for their hard work and passion. However, we should not forget and should be made aware of the bravery and selflessness that some of these women listed above displayed, and of course many others, when they travelled to Spain as nurses or as other volunteers like Ruth Ormesby, or those who were tireless workers in support of the Spanish Republic like Cora Hughes. When we Irish are called upon, both men and women, we never fail to rise to the occasion. What these women did, and the fact that it wasn't even their home country, is highly admirable and so that is where I got the inspiration to write this essay; as I believe that Irish women's tremendous work during the Spanish Civil War ought to be recognised and admired.

Muireann Hickey,
Coláiste Íde agus Iosef
Abbeyfeale
Co. Limerick

1: Irish Examiner Saturday 29th December 2012.

2: http://www.spartacus.schoolnet.co.uk/SPirish.htm

3: http://www.spartacus.schoolnet.co.uk/SPirish.htm

4: National Library of Ireland

5: http://irelandscw.com?misc-IWDUnity.htm

6: Ireland and the Spanish Civil War – Women and the SCW, Reprints pamphlet 5 by Dr. A Jackson & Ciarán Crossey

7: Irish Times on January 8th 2000

8: http://irelandscw.com/misc-IWDUnity.htm

9: http://ucdhiddenhistory.wordpress.com/2009/11/29/ucd-the-spanish-civil-war/#ref6

Spain's Civil War Legacy

by Michelle O'Donnell

A Limerick woman may not have fought against Franco in the Spanish Civil War. However, one remarkable Limerick woman, Kate O'Brien, captured the agony of Spain wrenched apart and destroyed by the evil fascist dictatorship of General Franco. *Farewell Spain,* first published in 1937, is O'Brien's elegy to her beloved Spain and the book's overt anti- Franco theme earned her a ban from the country until 1957 (O'Brien, 2006, xiii). O'Brien chose a pen as her weapon against fascism, but thousands of Republican women fought in more traditional ways.

There are two Spanish Holocaust survivors remaining alive - Conchita Grangé Veleta better known as Conchita Ramos (the name she used in the camps) and Neus Català, each suffering with health conditions and memory problems. Politically, the approach to Holocaust remembrance began to change in Spain as it became part of parliamentary and public discourse. On the other hand, Spain's conservative Party Popular (PP), who have publically tried (and failed) to distance themselves from Franco's right-wing conservatism, hold a different view on Spain's historical memory. Georgina Blakeley, who has written extensively on Spain's Historical Memory Law and on Spanish democratization, concludes that, 'The Law of Historical Memory is, therefore, more important for what it symbolizes politically than for its legal consequences' (Blakeley, 2008, 324). This is due to the veiled support PP has given to this law. Thankfully, this is not something the Spanish government can continue to get away with. The United Nation's committee on Human Rights and Torture and their Working group on Forced and Involuntary Disappearances have both criticized Spain for failing to repeal the 1977 Amnesty Law and failing to fully fund the Historical Memory Law (Garzón, 2013). The UN Committee on Forced Disappearances demands that Spain does more to locate the mass graves of the Civil War dead, calling for the immediate:

> adoption of the necessary legislative and judicial measures, with a view to overcoming legal obstacles of a domestic nature that may impede such investigations, particularly the interpretation given to the Amnesty Law (Garzón, 2013).

According to Blakeley:

> The Association for the Recovery of Historical Memory estimates that approximately 30,000 non-identified bodies, killed between 1936 and 1977, lie in common graves across Spain, including the most famous disappeared person of all, Federico García Lorca[1] (Blakeley, 2005, 57).

The exact number of Spain's disappeared and those who remain buried in mass graves (including Lorca) is impossible to calculate (Preston, 2013). Baer argues that locating mass graves is essential in order for Spain to move forward: 'The "recovery" of the memory fundamentally entails the exhumation and identification of bodies from mass graves, as well as commemorative ceremonies, cultural initiatives, and investigations of the victims of Franco's regime' (Baer, 2011,116). It remains a contentious issue in Spain.

For many in Spain, Franco, the fascist dictator, continues to enjoy what Preston describes as 'relatively good press', due to 'a series of persistent myths about the benefits of his rule' (Preston, 2013, xii). A major trope of Francoist propaganda was that Franco single-handedly saved Spain from a 'Jewish-Bolshevik-Masonic conspiracy' while keeping Spain out of the World War II and that he revived the Spanish economy in the 1960s (Preston, 2013, xi-xii). This is certainly evidenced in the policies and attitudes of Spain's right-wing conservative Party Poplar (PP) and their reluctance to commemorate the Holocaust in Spain and to act on the future of the Valley of the Fallen (Valle de los Caidos)[2]. The Valley of the Fallen is a huge monument/ memorial located in the Guadarrama Mountains at San Lorenzo de El Escorial outside Madrid. It was commissioned by General Franco himself to commemorate the Civil War dead, and is the site of the dictator's grave, and also interred there is Primo de Rivera, founder of the Falange. The site is hugely controversial and contentious in contemporary Spain. Thousands of Republican victims of Franco were buried in a mass grave at the site, and thousands perished during its construction (Preston, 2013, 509). The future of the site remains in limbo and is the focus of an ongoing bitter debate within Spain (Rainsford,

Valle de los Caídos; Valley of the Fallen
Basilica & Memorial & burial place of Franco

2011). Each year a commemoration mass is celebrated for Franco and the site itself remains adorned with fascist symbolism which Abend describes as:

> from the Pieta at the foot of a massive, 490-foot cross, to the looming statues of crusaders that line the walls of the underground basilica — were emblems of the dictator's National Catholicism, the Valley of the Fallen has always been closely identified with the war's victors. The presence there of the tombs of both the founder of Spain's fascist party and Franco himself only reinforce that association. (Abend, 2010).

In 2013, Odón Elorza, a member of Spain's Socialist Party (PSOE) forwarded a bill proposing the exhumation of Franco's body from the site to be reinterred in the family grave or to a 'more appropriate' site (Hamilos, 2013). The Bill also calls for the site to become a place of cultural reconciliation and collective memory for all Spaniards, but as Hamilos notes 'the bill will now have to be voted on by a parliamentary commission, where it is likely to face opposition from the governing rightwing People's party' (Hamilos, 2013). The site is viewed by many as 'a rallying point for the far right' (Rainsford, 2011). The controversy over Spain's largest Francoist memorial is one which is set to continue for the foreseeable future and one which unfortunately, the remaining Spanish Holocaust survivors may not live to see reconciled.

The Valley of the Fallen may be Spain's largest Civil War memorial; however it is not the only memorial at the centre of controversy. In 2013, lawyers for Spain's PP party called for the removal of a memorial from the grounds of Madrid's Complutense University on the basis that it violated planning regulations (Mathieson, 2013). The memorial is dedicated to the International Brigades, the volunteers from all over the world who went to Spain to fight in the Civil War (ibid). The memorial itself is a 'simple metal column' with a small inscription and was funded by private donations. It stands in the University grounds, which was a stronghold of anti-Fascist support during the Civil War (ibid). According to Mathieson:

> Popular Party (PP) that runs the city is not prepared even to tolerate its existence…it now seems that political spite will do away with the only commemorative plaque to the International Brigades in the entire city…it is often said that history is written by the winners. But what is happening in Madrid is not just an asymmetrical exercise of historic

Memorial to the International Brigades at Madrid's Complutense University

memory. It is an intolerant, dangerous, dysfunctional way to treat the past and sits uneasily with the image Madrid likes to project as an open, diverse and transparent city of the future (Mathieson, 2013).

It is highly significant that a memorial to the Limerick men who fought Franco is being erected in Limerick City. Kate O'Brien would be extremely proud of the men and women who continue to honour those who risked all to fight against evil. It is ironic that in Spain today the issue of Civil-War memorialisation is a contentious and current topic: Republican memorials are being ripped down in the heart of the Spanish capital, Madrid, while one is being erected in the small city of Limerick, far from the Spanish mainland. The last remaining statue of General Franco was only removed from the Spanish mainland in 2008, 33 years after the dictator's death (Govan, 2008). The statue was a 20 foot tall equestrian styled statue (ibid). Govan writes that a 'similar statue was removed from a square in the Spanish capital in 2005. It had served as a rallying point for pro-Franco supporters in Madrid and was dismantled in the middle of the night to avoid protests' (Govan, 2008).

It is very difficult to see how adequate representation can be given to Spanish survivors in Spain when its own government allows petty partisan politics to be used to settle old scores. If the PP act like this to a relatively small Civil War Memorial, the bigger issue of the future of the Valley of the Fallen is not likely to be resolved any time soon or satisfactorily.

Modern Spain remains in an historic memory vacuum because the country has never gotten to grips with its post-Civil War past, which is evidenced by the fact that the 'consequences' of the war continue to 'reverberate bitterly in Spain today' (Preston, 2013,). Thousands of Republicans and anti-Franco supporters fled or were exiled from Spain during and after the Civil War (1936-1939). Many joined the French Resistance in the fight against fascism (Preston, 2013, 515). Due to Hitler's and Franco's allied status, a large number of Spaniards were sent to German concentration camps and experienced the full horrors of the Nazi concentration camp system. Among them were a group of women. Paul Preston estimates that, 'in Ravensbrück, there were 101 Spanish women who had belonged to the French Résistance' (Preston, 2013, 515). Ravensbrück was a women's concentration camp north of Berlin in Germany.

Women were singled out and subjected to the full extremes of the Franco regime, Republican women in particular. Once in power, Franco and his Falange party went about dismantling the structure of the Republican government and he introduced the Napoleonic Civil Code which, 'legally imposed women's subordination to men in all spheres of life, denying the former their most basic rights and autonomy as individuals' (Tsuchiya, 2003, 212). Women were denied rights and a voice under Franco. Both Franco and his wife, Carmen Polo, were devout Catholics, with his wife being particularly fanatical in her devotion. Spanish women, in particular, were expected to live their lives in accordance with strict Catholic mores (Preston, 2013). The experiences of women in Nazi concentration and labour camps have been well documented and the Spanish political prisoners sent to Nazi camps would have endured likewise. However, the fate of political prisoners in Franco's Spain was not much better. Rape, branding 'with Falangist symbol,' [3] forced adoption of Republican children and summary executions were among the worst punishments inflicted on women (Preston, 2013, 511). The brutality and deprivations endured by female Republicans are epitomised in the story of Las Trece Rosas (The Thirteen Roses). In August 1939, a group of fifty-six political prisoners were executed. Among the group were 13 women (the majority under twenty-one years of age) and a young boy (Preston, 2013, 512). Las Trece Rosas have come to symbolise the 'cruelty of the Franco Regime' (Preston, 2013, 512). One well-documented atrocity is that of Amparo Barayón who was executed in 1936 for being a Feminist and wife of a Republican sympathiser (Preston, 2013, 511). Her infant daughter had been ripped from her arms the previous day by a prison guard and placed in an orphanage (ibid). Therefore, the Spanish political prisoners liberated from Nazi camps in 1945, were unable to return to Spain until Franco's death in 1975 because of the abuses they potentially faced in Franco's prison system as female Republican sympathisers.

The repressed female voices of Spanish Holocaust survivors and Republican political prisoners in general are slowly beginning to be heard. This has been a long and protracted denial of human rights orchestrated by Franco's fascist regime and carried on in the policies and ideologies of the right-wing PP party. For decades, these women were written out of Spain's official history and are still struggling to be fully included. There exists in Spain a chronic lack of political will demonstrated by Spain's conservative Party Popular (PP) to adhere to United Nation's Committee on Enforced Disappearances and UN committees on Human Rights and Torture. They have allowed Spain to be criticized and admonished by UN and the world at large for their failure to act decisively in locating and opening Civil War mass graves and to adequately finance and support Spain's Historical Memory Law. The distortion and erasing of history by PP and not allowing women equal rights and agency is an ideological legacy going back to the party's origins in the Falange party. These examples are paradigmatic of a view held by many in Spain that Franco was a great man and what he achieved is something Spain should be proud of. Also, the internecine political issues and pettiness that are preventing Spain's politicians from working as a united force to acknowledge and accept its recent violent history and to help their country move forward and not move backwards.

Spanish Holocaust survivor stories do not form part of any national school curriculum and the history of the Civil War is not taught in an open and useful way. There is only one small museum in Catalonia, the Museu Memorial de l'Exili (The Exile Memorial Museum) dedicated to those exiled from Spain during Franco's reign of terror. As yet, their stories are not fully integrated into Spain's official history. This is a consequence of how the Holocaust and the Civil War are remembered in contemporary Spain. The continued exclusion of female perspectives on Spanish history is a shame on Spain.

For Spanish Holocaust survivors, their war did not end with liberation from Nazi concentration camps in 1945. For many, their war began with the death of General Franco in 1975 because it was then that their battle for identity and representation in their homeland truly began. The battle continues and once the last remaining female survivor dies, then their crusade for justice will be continued by their descendants, friends and dedicated historians like Montserrat Llor. Kate 'O Brien fell in love with Spain as an outsider just as I have done. O'Brien was an outspoken critic of Franco and in her 1937 elegy Farewell Spain she captures the final moments of pre Civil-War Spain, she writes 'Spain at the Cease Fire, if it ever comes, will have a very difficult garden to cultivate' (O'Brien, 2006, 224). Sorry Kate, but we are still waiting for the full bloom.

¡No Pasarán!

Exile Memorial Museum, La Jonquera

Endnotes

1: Spanish poet and dramatist assassinated by Francoist henchmen and buried in an unmarked grave in 1936.

2: The Valley of the Fallen is the vast monument General Francisco Franco commissioned to commemorate his victory in the Spanish Civil War.

3: Name of Franco's Fascist Party whose symbol was the Yoke and Arrows.

Bibliography

A View of Madrid (2009) 'Madrid Holocaust Memorial' (Blog Post) [Internet] http://aviewofmadrid.blogspot.ie/2009/01/madrid-holocaust-memorial.html [Accessed 27 February 2014].

Abend, Lisa (2010) 'Should Spain Close Franco's Tomb?' [Internet] http://content.time.com/time/world/article/0,8599,2032400,00.html [Accessed 30 March 2014].

Amical Ravensbrück (2014) [Internet] http://www.amicalravensbruck.org/reportaje.asp?id_rep=1 [Accessed 23 April 2014].

Baer, Alejandro (2001) 'Consuming history and memory through mass media products'. *European Journal of Cultural Studies* 4 (4), pp. 491-501.

Baer, Alejandro (2011) 'The Voids of Sepharad: The Memory of the Holocaust in Spain'. *Journal of Spanish Cultural Studies* 12 (1) pp. 95-120.

Català, Neus (1984) De la Resistencia y la Deportación: 50 Testimonios de *Mujeres Españolas*. Adgena: Barcelona.

Garzón, Baltasar (2013) 'Can Spain Face the Truth' [Internet] http://elpais.com/elpais/2013/12/02/inenglish/1385992104_683721.html [Accessed 23 March 2014].

Govan, Fiona (2008) 'Last statue of dictator removed from mainland Spain' [Internet] http://www.telegraph.co.uk/news/worldnews/europe/spain/3832807/Last-statue-of-dictator-Franco-removed-from-mainland-Spain.html [Accessed 12 January 2014].

Llor, Montserrat (2014) *Vivos En El Averno Nazi*. Barcelona: Editorial Planeta.

Mathieson, David (2013) 'Madrid's dangerous attempt to distort the history of the Spanish civil war' [Internet] http://www.theguardian.com/commentisfree/2013/jun/06/madrid-history-anti-fascist-resistance [Accessed 26 March 2014].

O'Brien, Kate (2006) *Farewell Spain*. London: Virago

O'Donnell, Michelle (2014) 'Giving a voice to the silenced: The under-representation of non-Jewish women in Holocaust memorials and museums in Spain'. MA Dissertation: Postgraduate Diploma / Masters Degree in Interpretation, Representation and Heritage by Distance Learning: University of Leicester.

Osborne, Raquel (2011) 'Good Girls Versus Bad Girls in Early Francoist Prisons: Sexuality as a Great Divide'. *Sexualities* 14 (5), pp.509-525.

Preston, Paul (2013) *The Spanish Holocaust: Inquisition and Extermination in Twentieth-Century Spain*. London: Harper Press.

Tremlett, Giles (2013) 'Spanish civil war monument must be pulled down, court rules' [Internet] http://www.theguardian.com/world/2013/jun/05/spanish-civil-war-monument-court [Accessed 26 March 2014]

Tsuchiya, Akiko. (2003) Women and Fiction in Post-Franco Spain. *The Cambridge Companion to the Spanish Novel*. Cambridge: Cambridge University Press.

From the Shannon to the Ebro

DE PROFUNDIS

From the Shannon to the Ebro

De Profundis

*Los cien enamorados
duermen para siempre
bajo la tierra seca.
Andalucía tiene
largos caminos rojos.
Córdoba, olivos verdes
donde poner cien cruces
que los recuerden.
Los cien enamorados
duermen para siempre.*

De Profundis

*Those hundred lovers
are asleep forever
beneath the dry earth.
Andalusia has
long, red-coloured roads.
Córdoba, green olive trees
for placing a hundred crosses
to remember them.
Those hundred lovers
are asleep forever.*

Federico García Lorca

Federico García Lorca was one of the most important Spanish poets and dramatists of the twentieth century, best known for his book of verse *Romancero Gitano* (The Gypsy Ballads) and the much-acclaimed play *La casa de Bernarda Alba* (The House of Bernarda Alba). He was born on 5 June 1898 in the province of Granada, the eldest of four children. Although more interested in music than in his academic studies, he attended the University of Granada's Faculties of Philosophy and Letters and of Law. However, his musical abilities continued to develop under the teaching of Don Antonio Segura. Through his poetry and plays, he became internationally-known and was a member of the *Generación del 27* which included Salvador Dalí and Luis Buñuel.

In 1931, he was appointed by the new left-wing Republican government as the Artistic Director of the Teatro Universitario, a touring theatre company which came to be known as 'La Barraca'. For the next four years, the company performed the great Spanish plays of the sixteenth and seventeenth centuries in the towns and villages of rural Spain as part of the government's broad-based educational programme. In 1936, with increasing political trouble in Spain, Lorca's socialist sympathies were increasingly in evidence. He was detained by Nationalist forces for two days before being murdered by them in August 1936. His books were burnt in Granada's Plaza del Carmen and were later banned from Franco's Spain. Sadly, to this day, it is not known where this great poet's remains are buried.

From the Shannon to the Ebro

CONTRIBUTORS

From the Shannon to the Ebro

CONTRIBUTORS

Richard Baxell

Richard Baxell is a research associate at the London School of Economics and a Trustee of the International Brigades Memorial Trust. He is the author of a number of books and articles on the British volunteers including the critically-acclaimed British *Volunteers in the Spanish Civil War*. His latest book, *Unlikely Warriors*, an oral history of the volunteers published by Aurum Press, was shortlisted for the 2013 Political Book Awards political history book of the year.

Jane Bernal

Jane Bernal is the daughter of Margot Heinemann and JD Bernal. She recently retired from being a Consultant in the NHS. She lives in Cornwall and is working on a full-length biography of her mother, Margot Heinemann.

Jack Bourke

Jack Bourke is a native of Limerick City and is now happily retired. A Chartered Accountant by profession, he formerly worked with Shannon Development Company and with the EU Commission in the area of Economic Development Policy. He is married to Phil and has three children and four grandchildren.

Melody Buckley

Melody Buckley, an American with a lifelong passion for history, has lived in Co Limerick since 1996. Her odyssey began when she first heard of the Limerick exploits of George Nathan at a lecture on the Spanish Civil War at the City Library. She went on to pursue and track down information about him on three continents. Her biography of George Nathan is a work in progress. In her other life, she is a student pursuing a PhD in Law and Psychology and the author of a decidedly non-historical book, *Civil Procedure and Practice*, published by Thomson Reuters in 2004.

Pamela Cahill

Pamela Cahill is a freelance writer and blogger living in Santander, Spain, where she has been based since 2007. She previously worked as a freelance journalist for travel, business and banking magazines in Amsterdam, Madrid and London. She has a BA (European Studies) with Spanish from the University of Limerick. In her free time she can usually be found reading a Kate O'Brien, rowing on the bay of Santander, or snooping around the food markets of Northern Spain.

Tom Collopy

Tom Collopy is a Company Director in Limerick City. He is an avid amateur student of Military History, particularly the involvement of Irishmen in foreign wars. He is a father of two sons and one daughter, and has an active interest and involvement in local politics and local issues. Tom is active in his residents' association, the Nicholas Street Residents and Business lobby, and is a member of the King's Island Adult Education Board.

David Convery

David Convery is an Irish Research Council Postdoctoral Fellow at the National University of Ireland, Galway. He completed his PhD in University College Cork in 2012 on the history and memory of Irish anti-fascists in the Spanish Civil War. He is the editor of *Locked Out: A Century of Irish Working-Class Life* (Dublin: Irish Academic Press, 2013).

Simon Donnelly

Simon Donnelly, from Limerick, studied engineering at L.I.T. and then went on to be awarded a first class honours B.A. degree in Fine Art at Limerick School of Art and Design. In 2012, Simon was nominated for The RDS Student Art Awards with his piece, Vorsprung Durch Angst. He was also awarded 'The Curator's Award' in the Limerick School of Art and Design Drawing Awards for his piece entitled 'Mr. Stillcry'.

Simon's work in visual arts has led him through post-production, editing, art direction, cinematography, set design and construction. He has worked with Limerick City of Culture on various projects, including Elemental Festival, Pig Town Fling and The Catch.

Using his knowledge and love for metalwork, he was honoured by the purchase of his piece 'Copper Heart' by the University of Limerick which is now on display on campus.

Emma Gilleece

Emma Gilleece is an historian specialising in early twentieth century architectural recording and building conservation. She received a BA in English & History (UL, 2007) MA History of Art & Architecture (UL, 2009) and MSc Urban & Building Conservation (UCD, 2011). She is Vice-Chair of the History & Heritage pillar for Limerick City of Culture and PRO for the Limerick Chapter of the Irish Georgian Society. She has been a member of the LIBMT committee since December 2013.

Muireann Hickey

Muireann Hickey is a native of Mountcollins,Co. Limerick,and is a student at Coláiste Íde agus Iosef, Abbeyfeale, She has a keen interest in history, and in February 2014 won first prize in the The Friends of the International Brigades Spanish Civil War Schools' Essay Competition. Her prize afforded her the opportunity to travel to Spain where she read her prize-winning essay at a commemoration ceremony in the historic Madrid Athenaeum.

John King

John King lives in Raheen, Limerick, is married to Kate and has three children, Stephen, Ann and Niamh. Previously employed by Shannon Development, he is currently CEO with the Irish Ancestry Research Centre in Limerick City.

Joe Malone

Joe Malone has written extensively in *The Old Limerick Journal* about the city of Limerick. He has broadcast on radio and television on the social, political and economic aspects of life in his native city. He is a well-loved character, possessed of abundant charm and wit. He ran a very popular hostelry in the city for many years. Long may he prosper!

Ger McCloskey

Limerick man, Ger McCloskey is an amateur historian specialising in the Spanish Civil War and particularly the International Brigades and the P.O.U.M. Married to Anne Madden, they have 2 grown up children, David and Katie, and live in Broadford, Co, Clare.

Mike McNamara

Mike McNamara, a Brick & Stonelayer by trade, is a full-time Trade Union official with more than 16 years experience representing workers and their families. Mike is the President of the Limerick Council of Trade Unions, the umbrella body of the Trade Union movement in Limerick. He is also the Secretary of the Limerick Mechanics' Institute Delegate Board and an amateur historian, with special interest in the Guilds of Limerick and the "Limerick Soviet 1919". He is married to Rose and lives in Limerick.

Michelle O'Donnell

Michelle O'Donnell, originally from Pallasgreen, Co. Limerick, now lives in Almeria, Spain. She holds an MA from Leicester University in Interpretation, Representation and Heritage.

Ruan O'Donnell

Dr. Ruan O'Donnell is a Senior Lecturer in History at the University of Limerick. A former Visiting Chair of Irish Studies at the Keugh-Naughton Institute, Notre Dame, he is the author of numerous publications on the history of Irish republicanism including 'Special Category, The IRA in English Prisons, 1968-1978'.

Manus O'Riordan

Born in Dublin in 1949, Manus O'Riordan is Ireland Secretary of the International Brigade Memorial Trust, an Executive Member of Friends of the International Brigades in Ireland, and son of the Cork-born Connolly Column International Brigade volunteer and historian, Micheál O'Riordan (1917-2006), the second expanded edition of whose book, *Connolly Column*, he edited in 2005.

From 1971 to 2010, Manus served with the ITGWU and SIPTU as the Union's founding Head of Research, and, since 2010, has been a Member for Ireland of the Workers' Group of the European Economic and Social Committee.

Manus was an Executive Member of both the Connolly Youth Movement in the 1960s and the British & Irish Communist Organisation in the 1970s, and, in 1982, he became a founding member of the Democratic Socialist Party, led by the Limerick Socialist TD and future Mayor of Limerick, Jim Kemmy (1936-1997).

Manus graduated from University College Dublin in 1969 with a BA in Economics and Politics, and from the University of New Hampshire in 1971 with an MA in Economics and Labour History, inclusive of a thesis, *Connolly in America*, subsequently published by Athol Books in 1971. Manus is the author of *Connolly Socialism and the Jewish Worker* (Irish Labour History Society, 1988); *Communism in Dublin in the 1930s: The Struggle against Fascism* (in H Gustav Klaus, ed, Strong Words, Brave Deeds, O'Brien Press, 1994); *The Voice of a Thinking Intelligent Movement: James Larkin Junior* (Irish Labour History Society, 1995); *Larkin in America: The Road to Sing Sing* (in Donal Nevin, ed, James Larkin: Lion of the Fold, Gill & Macmillan, 1998); and *James Connolly Re-assessed* (Aubane Historical Society, 2006). Manus was also the editor of both The American Trial of Big Jim Larkin (Athol Books, 1976) and *Irish Solidarity with Cuba Libre: A Fenian Eyewitness Account of the First Cuban War of Independence* (SIPTU, 2009), as well as being co-editor with Francis Devine of *James Connolly, Liberty Hall & the 1916 Rising* (SIPTU, 2006).

Danny Payne

Danny Payne, a Trade Union activist from Liverpool has been working to preserve the memory of those from Liverpool and the surrounding area who fought in the Spanish Civil War.
He has over the years produced exhibitions and events around the theme of "Liverpool and the Spanish Civil War" to keep the memory of their sacrifice alive and sees the struggles of the 1930s as not a dusty historical episode, but part of our collective ongoing struggle for political change and social justice.
He is currently studying for a degree in History, firstly at Ruskin Collage Oxford and currently at Liverpool University

Alan Warren

Alan Warren is a British historian living permanently in Barcelona studying the International Brigades in the Spanish landscape. He has appeared in numerous television documentaries concerning the Spanish Civil War, and the forthcoming *War is Beautiful* documentary, based on the diaries of ambulance driver James Neugass, will be premiered in Autumn 2014. Alan conducts tours of the Battlefields of Spain for families of International Brigaders and students studying the conflict. For details of his current research go to www.pdlhistoria.wordpress.com.

Bill Watkins

Bill Watkins was born in 1950 into a Welsh/Irish family. Both of his parents were bilingual as well as notable traditional singers. As a teenager, he tramped the roads of the British Isles and Europe in the wake of his heroes, W. H. Davies, Welsh poet and author of *The Autobiography of a Super-Tramp* and Eric "Burton" Blair who later rose to fame as the English writer and socialist, George Orwell. Bill is also an accomplished singer/songwriter whose most famous ditty *The Errant Apprentice* has been recorded worldwide. Now living in Minneapolis, Minnesota, he entertains as a publican and free-lance druid.